MW00937014

Living Beyond the Sunset

A story of love, loss, and resilience

Leah Compton Goodman

Copyright © 2018 by Leah Compton Goodman

All rights reserved.

Author's Note: This book is a memoir. It is my best effort to recreate as accurately as possible – my life.

Grateful acknowledgment is made to Pete Kartsounes for permission to print lyrics from his song: *While The Band Plays On*

Author's photograph by:
Kirk Shorte Photography, LLC

Front and back cover designed by:
Debbie Christiansen, DChristi Design

Front and back cover photographs by:
Courtesy of the author

Interior photos:
From the author's collection

Text set in Garamond

ISBN: 1983545430
ISBN-13: 978-1983545436

DEDICATION

In memory of Chad Goodman, my loving husband.
You left an imprint in all of our lives with your sense of humor, smile,
laugh, adventurous character, and endless storytelling.
You will always be remembered.

And he held on…

one more month,

one more week,

one more day,

one more hour,

one more minute,

one more second

… then he was done.

~Leah Compton Goodman

CONTENTS

CONTENTS

ACKNOWLEDGMENTS

A special thanks to my mom. Her presence and support was pure love, something only a mother could provide to her daughter.

To my soul sister… when my life erupted like a volcano, you were always there. You are very special to me, Lynne.

This book came about because of my editor, Beth Bornstein Dunnington. She gave me the courage and confidence to put pen to paper. "Just start writing," she said.

I'm forever grateful to the beautiful Island of Hawaii. You embraced me with open arms and taught me there was life after death. Upon my arrival I was broken and didn't know if I could put myself back together, but you restored my soul, my confidence, and my love for life.

Mahalo to Pele for giving me the opportunity to heal while surrounded by the spiritual grandeur and beauty of the islands.

I would like to express my greatest gratitude to my family, friends, and many acquaintances who helped us through this difficult time. For all the times you lent a hand to Chad and visited him, I thank you from the bottom of my heart. I treasure the laughs, smiles, cries, hugs, and the love you so generously shared with us. Each of you is a bright light; you nourished my soul and helped resuscitate life back into my limp body.

Rose Compton
Joel and Paula Compton
Jenna and Jonathan Compton
Patricia Goodman
Lisa Goodman and Drew Fennell
David Goodman

Mary Nash, Witt, and Caroline Godden
Todd and Donna Goodman
Daniel and Brooke Goodman
Eric and Cathy Goodman
Anna and Amy Goodman
David Castaldo
Joe Castaldo
Kay Castaldo
Lynne and Bob Bird
Brian Vinski
Matt Stover
Lance Fargo
Steve Barnett
Aileen Balitz
Kathy Barany
Susan and Stuart Frank
Lisa Nardone
Terry and Karen Engels
James Frash
Sean Quinn
Father Lou
Candace Lawrence
Annie Gleason
Ed Godden
The doctors and staff at Crouse Hospital
The doctors and staff at Hematology-Oncology Associates of CNY
The doctors and staff at Fox Chase Cancer Center
The staff at Hospice of Central New York
The staff at The Centers at St. Camillus

INTRODUCTION

Each day on this earth the sun rises and falls. Some days you can see the bright glow that ascends into morning haze, other mornings you can't see it for the dark stormy current churning through the air.

A sunset has always been the highlight of my day. I have pulled over on the side of the road to watch. I have put together an entire evening with a blanket, chair, dinner, and drinks at my favorite place to watch the yellow blaze disappear beyond the horizon. This event connects to a strong feeling deep inside me, the finality of the day being over. You can't go back and change or take back anything you said or did or maybe didn't do. It's a time for reflection. It's a time to be grateful. The sun shines splendor down on all things.

No matter how beautiful or gloomy the day begins, it continues to progress. Morning to afternoon to evening, then the day fades into night. At some point in our lives a dark cloud may roll in, as it did for me. None of us is immune.

My story is about love, loss, and how I came back to love life once again. Finding that sunrise was a glorious adventure. It doesn't have to take place halfway around the world, but can be found under a tree at a local park, in a cozy chair in your home, or conversing with a close friend. I took my healing and finding myself to the ultimate extreme because that's what I needed; it called to me. What I want is for each person to discover their own way.

Chapter 1

WAS THIS REALLY HAPPENING?

A day that forever changed my life.

It was New Year's Day 2011 and my husband Chad and I had just returned home after celebrating our godson's fifteenth birthday. Chad had been complaining for a couple of weeks about pain in his right shoulder, but today it was worse. I asked him if he wanted to go to the emergency room.

"No, I'll wait until my doctor's office opens after the holiday.

Not long after going to bed that night, Chad started tossing and turning. He let out a loud sigh every time he moved; he was extremely uncomfortable. After listening to this for a few minutes, I got out of bed, took off my pajamas, and put on jeans and a sweatshirt. I walked over to Chad's side of the bed and tapped him on the shoulder.

"Get up, I'm taking you to the emergency room."

He didn't resist, but I knew he wasn't happy about going. He didn't want my help as he slowly struggled to put on his clothes.

The hospital was about a fifteen-minute drive and there was no traffic at 11:00pm, but it seemed to take forever. Chad and I were no strangers to the emergency room... back pain, kidney stones, urinary tract infections. This was just another simple trip to the hospital, right?

The ER was packed. We sat down across from a prisoner who was handcuffed and shackled with a police escort. I looked around the room: there were young people, elderly folks, mothers, fathers, kids. Clearly, sickness did not discriminate.

My attention was drawn back to Chad, as he repeatedly stood and altered his weight from side to side. He took a few deep breaths and then sat down. After waiting for over an hour, his name was finally called.

"Chad Goodman."

We were shown to a stretcher in the hallway, where Chad sat down. The long hallway was lined with waiting patients and family members. What was going around, the flu? The doctor spoke to Chad briefly about his issue and ordered an x-ray of his right shoulder. Chad was wheeled away, but returned within a few minutes. Was there an emergency and patients were backlogged? Or was it just a busy winter night in the ER? I'd never seen so many people waiting to see a doctor.

Finally, the results.

They were inconclusive, but showed something suspicious in the apex of his right lung. The doctor ordered a CT scan of his chest and abdomen. When Chad returned from the scan we were ushered into a private room. The doctor entered and questioned Chad extensively about his travels abroad and what he may have been exposed to.

"When were you in Russia? What areas of Russia? When were you in South Africa? What parts of South Africa? What shots have you had? Were you sick while you were away or after you returned home?"

When the doctor left the room, Chad and I just looked at each other and didn't say a word.

My thoughts shifted to when he came home from the Limpopo Region of South Africa, only four months earlier. Chad called when he landed at JFK airport. He sounded terrible: hoarse, congested, coughing. He said he felt awful… had the chills, sore throat, was fatigued. He hadn't felt this bad in a long time.

I was concerned. What if he had contracted some weird disease?

When Chad arrived home he was pale, his eyes dark, and his shoulders were hunched forward. I immediately called his doctor and got an appointment for later that afternoon. As Chad sat on the examining table, the doctor checked every orifice, listened to his chest and back, and reviewed his vitals. "Are you a smoker?" she asked.

Chad was surprised. "Never."

"Wow, your lungs sound like a lifetime smoker in their seventies."

We were both shocked.

The doctor ordered a breathing treatment and after twenty minutes Chad's lungs sounded clearer. She wrote several prescriptions and sent him home to rest.

Suddenly, the door swung open and three emergency room medical professionals marched into Chad's room. I assumed they were in training; and why so many people?

The doctor had received the results of Chad's CT scan and explained to us that there was a tumor in the apex of his right lung, another tumor further down in his lung closer to his heart, and suspicious spots on his liver. We both listened intently as the doctor said, "We're admitting you to the

3

hospital for further evaluation."

I watched in disbelief as medical staff pushed my husband out of the ER and toward the elevator.

"Let's not jump to conclusions," I said, trying to put words to this. "You'll have some tests and then we'll see what we're dealing with."

I was confident it was something he picked up in South Africa.

We couldn't possibly know what the next two days would bring... they were a blur of MRI's, another CT scan, a bone scan, tons of lab work, and a biopsy of the mass. I escorted Chad to each test. I still refused to believe that something serious was going on. Chad was healthy, worked full time, was a black belt in karate, he was even studying for his nursing home administrator's license. He wasn't sick.

On the third day, the hospital generalist entered Chad's room, and sat down next to his bed. The chart in his hand was several inches thick. He opened it and confirmed our worst nightmare. "Chad... you have cancer that has spread throughout your body.

God, no.

"It's in your lung, spine, hip, brain and possibly your liver. I'm calling an oncologist." The doctor left. This had to be a dream, a nightmare, and any moment I would wake up. When the oncologist came into Chad's room later that evening I immediately disliked him. If for no other reason than the fact that he was the one delivering terrible news.

"You have lung cancer that has spread."

Please let me wake up from this nightmare.

"Pathology shows Stage IV with seven brain metastases and there's no surgical fix."

Then words like radiation and chemotherapy, pain regimen at home.

"Relief may take two to three weeks."

The next words were distorted, as if I was hearing them under water.

"Our ability to slow down the cancer is limited, only forty percent successful."

Time stood still. I could see the doctor's mouth move and the toneless sound slowly flow off his lips... cancer, Stage IV, brain tumors. I know there were other words but I lost the ability to hear anything he said after that.

I held it together in front of Chad, but I was falling apart. I was lightheaded as I stumbled down the hall to the bathroom, locking the door behind me. My lifeless upper body draped over the top of my thighs as I sat on the toilet. My chest was heavy; I gasped for air. My body trembled as I opened my clammy hands and placed my palms over my face. Tears soaked my fingers. My breathing shifted, as if I had a spasm or hiccups. As I stood up and shuffled towards the door, my knees buckled. I stopped and gazed into the mirror. How long had I been in there? I needed to go back to Chad. "Be strong," I said to myself.

"Be strong for Chad."

I left him alone in the hospital that night. He didn't want me to stay, maybe he needed time alone and maybe I did too. I went home and crawled into our bed. It was cold. Most nights I snuggled up to Chad. He'd lay on his back watching TV and I lay on my left side with my head buried in his armpit, my right arm stretched across his chest and my right leg thrown across his. Chad's body was always warm and I would frequently tell him, "You're like a furnace."

So here I was, alone in our bed. What just happened? I wanted Chad to be lying next to me. Chad was too young and had never smoked in his life. I had known two other people with lung cancer, co-workers. Both went through grueling treatment. Both took a handful of prescription drugs every day. Both wasted away to a skeletal frame. Both struggled and suffered. Both died. I didn't sleep that night.

The next morning Chad and I discussed his options. He could stay near home, go where there would be family support, or travel out of town to a large cancer hospital. A doctor friend of Chad's recommended he go where he had family and lots of support. So, Chad decided to get a second opinion from a small well-known boutique cancer center in Philadelphia, which was close to his family. We were surprised that he was able to get an appointment right away.

We loaded up the car and made the four-hour drive from Syracuse, New York to Wilmington, Delaware.

Over the next couple of weeks we stayed with Chad's mom in Wilmington and drove into Philadelphia several times a week. Chad saw various specialists who ordered additional tests to identify the particular type of lung cancer. The results would determine the treatment and the possibility of surgery. Once all the results were in, his primary oncologist would review them with us. I wanted a different answer than we got the first time, something less severe. In the back of my mind I still hoped for a strange disease from South Africa.

As we sat in front of the new doctor, it was déjà vu. There would be no waking up from this nightmare. Then the definitive news came.

"Chad, you have lung cancer that has spread from the original tumor to other parts of your body."

Chapter 2

TREATMENT?

Chad's team of Philadelphia doctors recommended radiation treatments first.

His radiation oncologist, a middle-aged female, treated all types of cancer, but had a particular interest in lung, brain, and spinal cord tumors. Dr. H had a patient-focused approach, which she described as each patient coming with a unique set of needs and concerns that she would address in the treatment plan. Sometimes the plan would be adjusted based on the patient's changing needs as treatment progressed.

Since Chad had metastases on his brain, Dr. H recommended whole brain radiation.

Whole brain radiation.

Chad's entire brain would be treated, not just the seven tumors. She explained that the short-term side effects could be uncomfortable – headache, hair loss, poor appetite, nausea, vomiting, fatigue, and skin changes on the scalp. The long-term side effects were more serious – trouble with memory, speech, and possible seizures.

Chad's eyes intently focused on Dr. H, his feet flat on the floor, and his upper body shifted forward in his seat. I scribbled as fast as I could in my notebook as she described the details of what could happen.

"Brain metastases are relatively common in lung cancer," she explained, "and the best job at controlling them is with radiation, because chemotherapy drugs do not cross the blood-brain barrier."

New words to learn, and our world was now filled with the stress and anxiety of medical stuff. Still, Dr. H had a positive outlook, at least for this portion of Chad's treatment.

Chad and I discussed the treatment and side effects as I drove back to his mom's house. He was never one to make a quick decision based on his gut instinct. He thought things through carefully, always weighing the pros and cons. I knew he was analyzing and evaluating every word he absorbed on that day. Chad could recall almost every detail of any conversation. That's why I took notes; I didn't have that gift.

On the drive, I kept most of my thoughts to myself. I was eager for him to begin treatment because I was confident he would have a positive outcome. I had faith. We had so much left to accomplish together; this was a bump in the road. In time, it would all be better.

The one thing I did say, "I support your decision."

The following morning Chad said, "I want you to shave my head. I don't want to wake up one morning with clumps of hair on my pillow."

My shoulders tensed as we set up shop in the bathroom. I'd never done this before, and had no clue as to what I was about to do. What if I nicked Chad's head? What if I hurt him?

Chad perched on a stool in front of the mirror with a white towel draped around his shoulders. I picked up the clippers and flipped the on switch; a high-pitched buzz filled the air. I looked at Chad in the mirror.

"Are you ready?"

He grinned slightly.

"Take a deep breath Leah, it'll be okay," I told myself.

I was uncertain about this job, but it couldn't be about me at this moment.

Chad didn't have much hair and it was already pretty short, but I cut it as close as I could to his scalp. Then I picked up a can of shaving cream and squirted white fluff into the palm of my hand and covered his stubbly head with it, putting a touch on his nose. He laughed as he wiped it away. After washing off my hands, I gripped a plastic disposable razor and placed it at his hairline near his forehead, and paused.

In a kind voice, Chad said, "Just do it."

I gently pulled the razor across the top of his head. It was a strange feeling... as if the blades were catching on his scalp, kind of a hesitation. I wanted to stop, but I didn't. This was a way to show my love and support. I placed the razor under running water to rinse off the residue, and continued until his head was smooth.

As I finished up, we caught each other's eye in the mirror and both smirked. Chad stood up and brushed his right hand over his bald head.

"Great job, Hon." I felt good. I gave Chad what he wanted. Tiny moments of success would have to sustain us for now.

The drive to Chad's first radiation appointment was long and quiet. I drove while Chad sat in the passenger seat and stared out the windshield. We were both scared, that fear of the unknown. Was this treatment going to help? Would he be in pain? What about the long-term side effects?

9

As we checked in at the front desk, the therapist was there, ready to take Chad back. This time, the first time, he allowed me to enter the treatment room with Chad during the set-up process.

I was grateful.

The room was large, and it swallowed up the massiveness of the radiation equipment. The walls were sterile white, but on the ceiling, above the equipment, was a piece of art. It was a recessed circular skylight, eight to ten feet in diameter, with four colorful stained glass windows separated by what appeared to be a large white wooden cross. Each smaller window was filled with a bright blue sky, scattered clouds, a few tree limbs, green leaves, and pink blossoms.

I held back the tears. This gave me hope: part of the tree dies off in winter, but flourishes a few months later. Chad would do the same.

My husband slowly walked towards the radiation machine and lay on his back with his arms down his sides. He'd been fitted for a treatment mask, which covered his entire face and forehead; it would hold his head still during treatment.

I watched as the therapist placed the mesh-like mask over his face and attached it to the table beneath him. Chad was restrained. Was this how it had to be? What if he panicked and needed to get up?

I walked over and touched his hand. "Love you!" I said trying to stay upbeat for him.

I was then politely asked to leave and shown the exit. As I closed the door behind me, my abdomen clenched tightly and I felt like I was going to throw up. I sat down in a chair and waited.

For the next ten days, powerful radiation was delivered to Chad's entire brain, and the same process repeated at each visit. The treatment made him extremely tired and he would often nap several times during the day. His choice of foods became very narrow: SpaghettiOs with meatballs, halvah, canned soups, and chocolate ice cream. He had always liked these foods, but they became his only source of calories for a couple of weeks, because that's what tasted good.

Sometimes he would crave certain foods like Steak-Umms, Snickers, Yoo-hoos, and then never have an appetite for them again. The kitchen counter was filled with half-empty boxes, cans, and bags of various foods. I bought everything he thought he might eat and expended my energy helping him in any way I could. I bought cookbooks for cancer patients, blended drinks with nutritional ingredients, and invited family over for meals, hoping he would eat with more people around.

Accompanying Chad to radiation every day made it real, and I slowly began to accept the circumstances. This was not an infection or disease he picked up in a foreign land. It was a serious illness with considerable consequences.

Many days I wished I had the power to blink my eyes and change everything, make it better, make 'it' go away. I could not say the word "cancer."

If I said it, it made it true.

Chapter 3

TREATMENT, PART II

Staying with Chad's mom was a great help. It was good to have the support from his family. His sister, Lisa, and her wife, Drew, lived two minutes away with their eleven-year-old son, David, and they would stop by most weekday evenings after work, often calling before leaving work to ask if they could bring takeout.

"What will Chad eat?" Lisa would ask.

His favorite was Walt's Fried Chicken in Wilmington; we ate it at least once a week.

Weekends were filled with even more family: Chad's older brother, Todd; his wife, Donna; and two young kids – nine-year-old Brooke and twelve-year-old Daniel; and Chad's younger brother, Eric; his wife, Cathy; and twin six-year-old girls, Anna and Amy.

The guys would talk about fishing trips they had taken, and they made plans to go to Cabela's when Chad felt better. Donna brought corn pudding, a favorite of Chad's. Cathy scanned the internet to find a recipe for a dessert with Keebler crackers that someone had once made for Chad.

The little girls (Brooke, Anna, Amy) would take turns sitting in Uncle Chad's lap and would sometimes fall asleep with their tiny heads lying on his chest.

Friends from high school visited frequently. Matt, Steve, and Chad had wrestled together back in the day, and they reminisced about their wild ways.

One time in particular, all three were skinny-dipping in the school pool during the wee hours of the night, when a patrolling police officer spotted them. They scattered like mice, and Chad hid behind a trash can in the back of someone's house. It was later determined it was Joe Biden's home. Obviously, this was many years before he became a well-known politician, but the three of them laughed and moved on to another story.

A college buddy, Brian, drove over frequently from Western Pennsylvania. Chad and Brian told stories and laughed. These two macho guys had once dressed as women in college and performed musical acts in front of a full audience.

As Chad visited with his friends, I watched from a distance. These were times to treasure and Chad cherished every moment with loved ones. It warmed my heart to see him smile and have some fun during such a difficult time.

We would not know the outcome of Chad's whole brain radiation for several weeks, and at this point the oncology team recommended he start chemotherapy.

He had blood drawn to make sure his body was strong enough for this new fight, and it was.

Chemo was a go.

Dr. B, Chad's primary oncologist, explained that treatments were life-long, two to three weeks apart, and the goal was to control the spreading of the disease to give Chad a better quality of life. He outlined the possible side effects:

fatigue, risk of infection, low blood cell counts, hair loss, rash, nausea, vomiting, loss of appetite, diarrhea, constipation, and numbness/tingling in hands and feet.

For his first treatment Chad chose to wear a blue t-shirt someone had given him, with a large Superman emblem on the front. It was perfect for the occasion. He would fight off the bad and become a hero.

Chad was viewed by family, friends, and coworkers as invincible, he *would* fight this and come out healthy again. We all thought that. He was confident and strong; there wasn't anything he couldn't do. Chad had a larger than life presence. When he walked into a room, his six-foot-two-inch muscular frame drew attention. His strong and confident voice pulled people in. They were impressed with his knowledge, his stories of his adventures, and his willingness to help others.

People came to Chad for help, but this time, he needed help.

We were escorted into the infusion room, to a large overstuffed lounge chair.

Another room to learn.

There was a television on a flexible arm and Chad moved it out of the way and sat down. I pulled up a small chair next to him and placed all my totes in the seat. You would have thought we were spending a few nights: bottles of water, snacks, movies, books, a computer, and my notebook. A nurse approached and took his blood pressure, pulse, temperature, and respiration rate, as I stood next to him and watched.

Chad would be given two drugs intravenously, through a port in his chest, which was implanted the week prior as an outpatient procedure. The oncology nurse hung clear plastic fluid-filled bags on a tall metal pole next to Chad. She reviewed the white label on the bags and glanced back at his chart. The nurse connected the ends of the bags to a long clear plastic tube and inserted the catheter into Chad's port.

The drugs would slowly drip into Chad's bloodstream for the next seven hours. During this time he remained tethered to the pole, the pole that held the drugs, the pole that may help save his life.

Chad seemed content. We talked, watched a movie, he read, and did a lot of texting. We both had hopes that the cancer was being killed off. We were optimistic Chad was going to be okay.

From the day of Chad's diagnosis, I felt like an actor in a movie. The director would eventually say, "That's a wrap" and we would go home to our normal life.

At other times I would beg God. "Please take us back! I'll do anything!" But in reality, I knew that could not happen.

I attempted to work some while Chad was going through treatment. But the day quickly came when I had to make an appearance in the office; some things couldn't be done long-distance.

It was just before Valentine's Day. As I left the pharmacy after picking up Chad's prescriptions, I noticed a small white teddy bear with a red heart sitting in a store window. A force beyond my control directed me inside, and I bought the bear. The morning I left Wilmington, I placed the teddy bear on my bed pillow, next to Chad. The thought of him being alone in bed made me feel sad. Heartbroken. He appreciated the gesture, but I knew he didn't want me to leave. Chad never told me this, but I knew he was more secure with me by his side. I took care of him and wanted the best for him. He always turned to me when he was asked a question like, "What medications are you on?"

"How's your appetite? When was your last treatment?"

I always had the answers in my notebook.

The drive back to Syracuse was difficult, I cried most of the way and felt as if I had abandoned Chad. He needed me and I needed to help him. But I would be back before his next chemotherapy treatment, I promised him that.

I was anxious to see my own primary care physician. My emotions were up and down like a destructive tidal wave. I felt mad and afraid, I trembled sometimes, and was constantly tired. I felt powerless and had trouble sleeping. When the doctor walked into the examining room I burst into tears. I was finally able to pull it together enough to tell her what was going on with Chad. She immediately wanted to prescribe an antidepressant. "But I'm not depressed," I said.

"I just feel numb and my chest is about to explode."

Was I trying to convince the doctor or myself that I wasn't depressed? Eventually she wrote me a prescription for an antidepressant and I took it. My next worry – Chad had a mass in his lung and no symptoms. I could have one too. Right?

My doctor said she understood my concern and ordered a chest x-ray. Was I rational? Was this a crazy thought? I shouldn't be thinking about myself; my husband was the sick one. I was confused and not sure about anything anymore.

Going into my office was tough. I didn't want people staring at me with their sad, feeling sorry-for-me faces. I didn't want pity, or anyone's sympathy. I was there to do a job and then go home, and that's all I wanted to do.

I purposely avoided people and worked at my desk with my office door partially closed. Most people were respectful of my space, which I appreciated. I didn't want to be there; my mind was on Chad. But I had to work. Two more days and I would be back with him. I was worried about how he was doing – did he feel alone, was he eating, did the teddy bear help at all?

Cancer cells grow and divide more quickly than normal cells, and chemotherapy drugs are made to kill growing cells. But healthy cells also multiply quickly, and chemotherapy can affect those cells too. The damage to the healthy cells is what causes side effects and everyone reacts differently. Even though Chad's side effects started with his second chemotherapy treatment, we remained positive and held on to the hope that treatment was destroying the bad stuff too. Dehydration was a serious side effect of chemotherapy because it robbed Chad's body of water and electrolytes through the vomiting, fever, sweating, and diarrhea he experienced, which compelled him to eat and drink less and less. I made every attempt to persuade Chad to ingest something... small bites, tiny sips, suck-on candy, ice, milk shakes, water, anything with fluid and calories.

I felt hopeless as my efforts were never enough. Chad continued to lose weight and became weaker.

In the midst of this storm came fantastic news – the seven brain tumors that had once thrived in Chad's brain were gone! A glimmer of hope I clung to for dear life... Chad's life. I was excited that the radiation blasted these suckers into oblivion, but Chad had no reaction. Did he somehow know? Did he have an idea what was really going on inside his body?

On top of the chemo, Chad also had major side effects from his oral medication, most significantly his pain medication, which alleviated his bone pain from the metastases. The doctor initially prescribed MS Contin, but quickly realized it made Chad extremely nauseous and caused violent vomiting spells. He had the same horrific reaction to Oxycontin and Roxanol.

The elimination process of pain medication was brutal on Chad. He carried a purple "puke bag," as he called it, everywhere. I found them in my car, on the nightstand, next to his lounge chair, and in his pants pockets. It was heartbreaking to watch his body wrench over the small plastic bag several times a day – during visits with friends, while relaxing in front of the television, or as a passenger in a car.

After weeks of trial and error, it was finally determined that he could tolerate Methadone. Why does an already sick person have to endure weeks of suffering – no appetite, weakness, vomiting? Then, much later, a resolution is determined. I am thankful for a resolution, but why does it take so long?

Dr. B recognized Chad had a double whammy. Chemo and pain medication made him feel so bad it was difficult for him to maintain an adequate intake of foods and fluids. He anticipated that intravenous (IV) hydration therapy would diminish some of the side effects and Chad would feel better.

"Better, what does that mean?" I asked.

He would apparently feel more energetic, rested, renewed, and refreshed. "Better" took on a whole new meaning for me. For the moment.

After three chemotherapy treatments and numerous admissions in and out of the hospital due to dehydration, the test results showed the cancer was still growing.

Dr. B informed us that only palliative care was available at this point, which meant there was nothing else they could do to stop/slow down the cancer.

What? Was this the end? How much time did we have? This was not fair. What did palliative care mean? Was I going to watch my husband die?

I wanted a fix. *Now*. Something that would help Chad, and take away his discomfort!

He could not continue this way, or was part of this that I could no longer watch? I felt helpless.

I scoured the internet for hours every day. Chad told me I was like a college student, always on the computer. I was looking for a miracle. My many hours of research led me to the latest medical journal articles, news reports, and clinical trials. I found two large research hospitals that were currently conducting clinical trials on Chad's type of lung cancer and I called both to discuss possible options for treatment. They requested medical information; I sent it and waited.

By the time Chad was considered for entry into a clinical trial, his condition had worsened and their determination was that he was not strong enough to participate. I was devastated. I should have done this sooner and I blamed myself for not doing so.

Chapter 4

AFTER TREATMENT

Chad made the decision that he wanted to return home to Syracuse, and we did.

He resumed his medical care with Dr. C, the same doctor who initially delivered the diagnosis four months earlier.

From the beginning of Chad's medical care in Philadelphia, his treatment notes were being sent to Dr. C. At his first office visit Dr. C said, "I want to make you as comfortable as possible by managing your symptoms."

He then recommended hospice.

As I opened the front door to our home, two young women stood side-by-side, one cradling a clipboard in her left arm, and the other clutching a black tote in her right hand. I greeted them with a smile, but it wasn't a display of how I really felt. I didn't feel anything. I was numb. An attempt to focus on the love and happiness was where I wanted to be, but was that possible? I kicked my feelings to the curb; it was the only way I could get through this.

My breath shortened as they entered. Both introduced themselves as I showed them to the living room, where Chad was seated in a lounge chair watching television. He picked up the remote and turned off the TV, then reached out to shake their hands. One asked, "How are you doing today, Chad?"

The other said, "We're here to admit you into hospice care."

A bomb dropped and our world continued to be blown to pieces. They asked a series of questions: What medications Chad was taking, did he have a Living Will and Health Care Proxy (both of which we had drawn up years ago when we did our wills), who were the friends and family members they could speak to about his medical condition? Every muscle in my body tightened as they discussed a Do Not Resuscitate Order (DNR). No mouth-to-mouth breathing, no pressure to his chest, no electric shock to re-start his heart, and no breathing tube to open his airways. If or when Cardiopulmonary Resuscitation (CPR) was needed, Chad would not receive it. There would be no bringing him back.

Chad was handed a clipboard with a form that he initialed and signed in several spots. What was going through his mind? I excused myself. If I hadn't, I would be a bumbling crying hunk of a human, and Chad didn't need to see that. He needed me strong. I slowly walked to our bedroom and grabbed a sweater from my closet. When I returned, they asked Chad if he had any questions. In a soft polite voice, he said "No, but thank you."

The next day medical supplies arrived: a tall metal IV pole, several large plastic bags filled with clear fluid, a box filled with individually wrapped alcohol pads, single prefilled shrink-wrapped syringes, and separately packaged disposable tubing. That afternoon a hospice nurse arrived to give me instructions on how to administer IV hydration therapy, which I had committed to the day before. I gathered the newly delivered supplies and set them on the bed next to Chad. I didn't give my mind the time for fear to set in; I just did as the nurse told me: "Put on gloves, hang a large fluid-filled bag from the pole, attach the disposable tubing to the bottom of the bag, make sure there are no kinks, and let the tubing hang."

The nurse said, "Leah, are you doing okay?" I nodded yes.

"Are you okay Chad?" she asked.

"Hopefully we don't have another Dr. Mengele here," Chad replied.

We both looked at him. I found it witty in an eerie way. The nurse continued... "Scrub the hub of the catheter (which was part of the port implanted in his chest) with an alcohol pad for thirty seconds and let it dry. Without setting the hub down, because it's now sterile, pick up a pre-filled syringe of heparin and remove the cap, connect the syringe to the hub, remove the clamp just below the hub, and slowly push the plunger until the syringe is empty. This will flush the line to ensure there is no blockage and reduce the chance of infection."

"You okay, Leah?" she asked again.

"Yes, I'm fine just focused."

Was there some strange look on my face? Did I look faint? Were my hands shaky? I didn't notice. She continued her instructions.

"Do not set the hub down, it's still sterile. Attach the disposable tubing to the hub."

The fluid began to slowly drip from the bag, through the tubing, and into Chad's vein. I was pleased, another job I could perform for my ailing husband.

Every day in the mail Chad received something uplifting... letter, postcard, box of goodies, card with lottery tickets, book, movie, audio book, or a small stuffed animal.

This was another escape for him, their good news and inspirational quotes. He knew people cared. As a reminder, I placed everything Chad was given around the house. The fireplace mantle was adorned with at least a hundred cards. A stuffed frog and teddy bear sat on the back of the couch. A blue three-ring binder, filled with pictures, notes, and poems sat on our coffee table. Chad felt the love. He was surrounded by abundant prayers and loving thoughts.

As a caregiver, all I could do was be there. Be present. My life was not mine, it was consumed by a situation that would end, and that's what I feared the most. I tucked my feelings inside, for the time being, because Chad was my focus. He didn't need the added stress of me being an emotional mess. This was my way to cope, and the best way for me to serve Chad and his needs. I would have time for myself later.

The Kentucky Derby was around the corner and it was an event we traditionally watched together. But this year I invited a few friends over and served one of Chad's favorites – pizza. Everyone sat with Chad and watched the pre-race festivities as I perfected the Mint Julep. It took me several tries, but I found the key was in the simple syrup. We all filled our plates with pizza and salad, grabbed a drink, and circled around the TV. As Bob Costas narrated the introductions of horse, jockey, owner, trainer, and farm name, Chad explained his history with horses. We all knew the story, but quietly listened as Chad told it again.

He had grown up on a horse farm. At one point it was the largest Trakehner (the oldest warmblood breed in the world) farm in the country. His family had a riding school, indoor arena, and over seventy-five horses they rented out. He pulled back his frail shoulders and his bony chest puffed out; he was very proud of all this.

David chimed in. "Yeah, remember the time we went bareback riding with only halters and lead shanks? We galloped down the side yard, spun the horses around, and yours took off towards the driveway." (Keep in mind the driveway was lined with huge pine trees). "Your horse went under one of the pines and the bottom branch caught you and pushed you off the horse. My horse followed, with the same outcome. We were lying on the ground, laughing.... it was lucky we didn't get hurt. What a great couple of horseman we were!"

The room filled with laughter, and I joined in.

I often encouraged Chad. "Did you take your medication? It's time for me to hook up your hydration therapy. Do you want a milkshake? Maybe some water, juice, or a Yoo-hoo? What would you like to eat? Tuna sandwich, peanut butter and jelly, mac 'n cheese?"

When I was on a roll with questions, he would often refer to me as Nurse Ratched. We would both laugh and I never gave it another thought. Yes, I attempted to pressure Chad, but I wasn't a battle-axe. My actions were an expression of love, as were his.

One day in the oncology office, I noticed a flyer on a bulletin board. "Lung Cancer Support Group meets once a month in Room 310 at 7 p.m., cancer patients, survivors, and families welcome." I mentioned it to Chad, and he agreed to attend.

We took the elevator to the third floor and Chad slowly walked to the end of a long hallway, where a small group of people gathered in a conference room. We entered and sat down at a large rectangular table that was covered with trays of wrap sandwiches, fruit, chips, and bottles of water. A nurse from Dr. C's office was present to answer questions or concerns that were brought up. She started with, "What's discussed in this room, stays in this room."

One by one we introduced ourselves and the patients and survivors briefly talked about their diagnoses. Each one had a different type: Stage II non-small cell, Stage 1 squamous cell, Stage IV adenocarcinoma, Stage II large cell, and Stage III bronchioloalveolar. My chest clenched when a middle-aged woman said, "One day we have a member, and the next meeting they're gone... they died. That's the tough part."

They all had varying degrees of the disease, but chose not to focus on the disease itself. They shared daily living challenges. "I no longer drive, I take time to nap, take care of myself... massage or reiki helps me, I no longer work, and how do I tell people no?"

I was drawn to one lady in particular – Julie. She was a four-year Stage IV lung cancer survivor. She didn't work, and had a hard time with friends and family wanting her to still do many things that she couldn't. "I may not look sick, but I am very sick," she said. "People don't understand the complexity of what's going on inside my body, and my mind."

After the meeting, I questioned Julie about her specific type of cancer, since she mentioned she had done so well with treatment. But her diagnosis was slightly different from Chad's. I used to think cancer was cancer, but there are so many details, variations, causes.

As best I understood, Chad's cancer began as a chromosomal rearrangement; he had an insertion and deletion mutation at exon 19 and 20. This is what I learned with all my internet research – technical terms and an exact understanding. It calmed my mind to know these details. On the drive home, Chad said, "Everyone doesn't work and I don't have to, it's okay to say no, if I want to sleep then I'll do it." I was happy.

Five months had passed since that shocking diagnosis and Chad was more fragile with each passing day. His face was thin and drawn, ribs and shoulder blades protruded from his back, ribs and collar bones stuck out from his chest, and his legs and arms were skeletal. He was so weak he relied on a cane, even around the house. I held my breath as he maneuvered from bedroom to living room to bathroom. I was horrified. If he fell, I was confident a bone would snap.

But I also wanted him to have some independence; I didn't want to hover, or for him to think I rendered him helpless, so I watched and prayed.

With the significant weight loss, Chad had a challenging time with his pants. So, I bought him two pairs of easy slip on/off, elastic waist, loose workout pants and a few smaller t-shirts. Chad went from an extra-large to a medium in only a few months. The disease was slowly taking him away from me, from our life, from his family, from this earth.

I felt crippled emotionally. I didn't eat right, felt exhausted most days, battled with headaches, and felt guilty I couldn't do more. I had no outlet. I discontinued my gym membership, no more running, and no respite. Any outside pleasure was out of the question. This was a demanding job, but I didn't care. I gave every ounce of energy to my husband, because that's what I wanted to do.

To give Chad variety in his sedentary day, and some form of exercise, I bought a Wii console. There were virtual games of tennis, bowling, car races, and target shooting. We each created a "Mii," a personalized avatar with facial features and a body type. The games provided low-level activity for his arms, eyes, and mind, which was better than sitting still all day. The more skilled Chad became, the more difficult the game. It challenged his brain. When we played against each other, we laughed, got disappointed over a dumb play, and celebrated wins with a high five hand smack. It brought excitement into our living room, and for the time being we didn't fear the future or think about Chad's illness. We enjoyed the moment.

My Mom and brother flew from Kentucky to visit for a long weekend. Joel, my brother, brought a small piece of red cloth with a tiny safety pin attached. His kids, Jenna (age fifteen, at the time) and Jonathan (age eleven) had made a small square prayer cloth, in hopes it would give their Uncle Chad comfort to know people were praying for him. He fastened it to his shirt and continued to wear it for weeks.

Neither Mom nor Joel had seen Chad since his diagnosis, but their relationship continued as normal. I never wanted Chad to be treated differently, for people to feel sorry for him or pity him. He would not have wanted that.

We laughed as we played board games, chatted with friends who came over for dinner, and sometimes just sat in silence. At the end of the weekend my mom said, "I'm not going home. I'm here to stay as long as you need me." I was grateful.

At night, the three of us would get ready for bed and Mom would crawl into our king-size bed with us, sometimes lying in the middle, and watch television. Chad would say, "I hit the mother-in-law jackpot." My mom smiled and patted his forearm.

She had visited us about a year ago and Chad took her to work with him one morning. One of her assigned jobs was pushing the elderly to and from the chapel for church services. When Chad brought her home at lunchtime her face lit up as she talked about how hard Chad worked, ran from one problem to another, and how helpful he was to everyone. "You know, as busy as he was he always made sure I had something to do, or someone to talk to," she said. "He's really good at what he does, so talented and smart."

As we lay in bed, I glanced over at my mom. She stared at Chad, and then I heard her say, "I'm lucky to have you as a son-in-law, and you and Leah are lucky to have each other."

Our house was chaos, mostly good chaos. The front door was always unlocked so friends and family could come and go. Chad loved having visitors and never turned anyone away. A carload of his coworkers frequently spent their lunch hour with Chad, talking, laughing, and bringing him up to date with work drama. They even Skyped him in for fundraising events and special parties.

Chad was vice president at a large healthcare facility that offered long-term skilled nursing care, short-term rehabilitation, and specialized care for brain injury, physical, occupational, and speech therapies, adult day health programs, nutrition services, and community education. There were over seven hundred employees. Chad had given fifteen years of his life to this facility, and loved it like he owned it. Most of the staff respected him. He held them accountable and motivated them to be the best at what they did. The staff was eager for him to return to work, but it was a topic we had never discussed.

Terry, a personal and professional friend, would stop by in the afternoon, sometimes staying to watch an entire movie. Susan and Stuart would bring lunch, and we enjoyed the special conversation of close friends. Kathy would never come into the house, but left donuts or pastries with whomever answered the door. Sean was a frequent guest, almost daily. He would bring a new-fangled tech gadget he had recently purchased, or discuss a new computer or phone he had his eyes on.

On one particular day, Matt drove up from Delaware, Steve flew in from Tennessee, and Lance stopped by after a dog competition in upstate New York. These three high school friends pulled chairs up next to Chad, who was propped up in bed, and reminisced.

Brian, Chad's friend from college, drove up for the weekend on at least two different occasions. Lynne, my best friend and a registered nurse, came by or called several times a day. She provided medical insight, fielded phone calls, and provided us with irreplaceable support, both emotionally and physically. Chad would joke daily, "When is 'LynneCare' coming over?" They had worked together and Chad talked about the fun they had in "bored" meetings and sometimes they would message back and forth to pass the time. He loved her.

David, Chad's best friend since age twelve, was a rock. He mostly visited on weekends and evenings, since he worked during the day. They would watch a movie, a TV show, talk, or just sit in stillness. At times, I thought they knew what each other was thinking. They were that close. Our house had a revolving door, but I would not have had it any other way.

Chad woke up one morning, gasping for every intake of air. I immediately called the doctor's office and they wanted to see him right away. I was terrified, but I gathered strength... the more stress I was under, the more focused I became. I hustled to get dressed and then pulled the car close to the front door. My arm was intertwined with Chad's as I escorted him out the door, down one step off the porch, and into the passenger's seat. He buckled himself in as my mom got into the back seat and I sat down in the driver's seat. I drove fast.

Once we arrived, Chad was rushed to an examining room. His vitals were taken and Dr. C appeared almost instantly. He placed his stethoscope on Chad's bone-riddled chest and listened to his lungs, then ordered a chest x-ray.

After reviewing the results, Dr. C explained Chad had a fluid build-up in the pleural membrane around his lungs and some of it needed to be removed. I watched as the nurse wheeled Chad down the hall and he disappeared around a corner. I returned to the waiting room where I had left my mom. I explained to her what was going on and the doctor said it would be a while – Chad had to get local anesthesia and the procedure was delicate. I'm not sure those were his exact words, but it had to be delicate, as a lung was involved. I sat quietly next to my mom and flipped through several magazines to keep my mind occupied, not reading one word. Finally, a lady at the front desk called my name. My heart sank... what did she want? As I approached she said, "Your husband is on his way out."

"Thank you," I replied. What a relief.

I stood at the doorway and waited. I could see Chad in a wheelchair down the hall. I smiled, but it quickly disappeared. Chad was slouched over and from a distance, his breathing sounded worse. I grabbed my purse and followed them, my mom right behind me, to a room with white curtained walls. I stepped out of the way as Dr. C and a nurse rushed in. The tears welled up as I stood in the distance and watched Chad struggle. His eyes bulged as he forced air into his lungs, and his chest looked heavy as the labored breathing caused his upper body to rise and fall by several inches. The fluid had constricted his airflow and there was a high-pitched wheezing sound as air attempted to pass through his lungs.

The medical professionals hovered over Chad. What were they doing? Help him! I felt lost and helpless… let ME do something. The nurse raised her head up and scanned the area, focusing on me. She dashed over. "You should call the rest of your family."

We called an ambulance. "Chad has a collapsed lung and will be admitted to the hospital," she said. "We don't think he has much time."

What did she just say?

I felt faint, weak in the knees. Nauseous. There was a tingling sensation that shot through my body. With a lump in my throat, I dug for my cell phone at the bottom of my purse and called Chad's sister.

Chapter 5

THE LAST THREE WEEKS

During the day, Chad's hospital room was a flurry of activity.

Nurses checked on his needs, aids changed his bed linen and brought fresh water, housekeepers emptied the trash, respiratory therapists checked his oxygen equipment, social workers asked if there was anything additional Chad or the family needed, pain specialists wanted to know his pain level on a scale of one to ten, nutritionists asked if there was something else he would eat, family was present, friends showed their compassion, and co-workers dropped by for a quick hello.

We all came to provide some level of comfort to Chad, and Dr. C was no exception. Dr. C was tall, slender, in his early fifties – an extraordinary doctor and person. One afternoon I asked him in the hallway, "How do you do this every day?"

"In the hopes that I can help someone."

Tears rolled down my cheeks. Chad was not going to be a success story. When Dr. C entered Chad's room it was like a superhero who swooped in to save the day. He brought joy to Chad. He would often pull up a chair next to Chad's hospital bed and they would swap fishing stories, discuss their passion for the Pacific Northwest, and compare favorite fishing spots.

One day Dr. C said to Chad, "I wish we would have met sooner and under different circumstances," and then he handed him a postcard of Mount Rainer, in Washington State.

There were daily comments from members of the medical staff on how much support Chad received from family and friends. Besides my mom, Chad's mom, and me, there was always someone else in his room, sometimes ten to twelve people at once. His room was filled with get well wishes, thinking of you cards, funny sayings, and jokes.

Two large collage frames that my brother brought from our home hung from the hospital wall. They were full of memories… Chad and me on our wedding day, Chad carrying Daniel on his shoulders at the New York State fair, Chad holding Anna in his right arm and Amy in his left arm when they were tiny babies, Chad and Jonathan displaying their catch after a day of fishing, Chad sending Jenna flying off his shoulders in my uncle's pool, Brooke sitting on Chad's lap while he wore her pink earmuffs, David and Chad geocaching at Rehoboth Beach, Chad and Joey (our godson) dressed in orange for his first hunting adventure, and various other family photos. Chad was surrounded by love.

There were people who visited that I never expected to see, like parents of children to whom Chad had taught ju-jitsu. They wanted him to know what a positive impact he had on their kids. Some people didn't come because they couldn't handle their own emotional stress about Chad's illness. Other people I thought would visit, or at least call or text, never did. I determined that people's true selves emerge in times of crisis, and at times it was disappointing.

One of Oprah Winfrey's quote sums it up: "Lots of people want to ride with you in the limo, but what you want is someone who will take the bus with you when the limo breaks down."

The days ran together; I couldn't keep track of weekdays versus weekends. The only thing I knew was that it was daytime or nighttime, simply because the sun radiated through the window blinds or it didn't. Some moments were clear and concise; others were hazy and difficult to remember. In general, I had a deep-down nervous feeling... what else could I do for him?

Every night I pushed an empty hospital bed next to Chad's, as close as I could get, and lowered my bed rails so I could get even closer. Rarely did anyone interrupt our night unless Chad's IV medication ran out, and the beeping noise from the monitoring device continued until a nurse exchanged it for a full one. By that point, I had watched enough times that I could now turn the beep off myself so it wouldn't wake him up, and then I would notify a nurse.

Chad slept quietly on his back with IV tubes connected to his port, oxygen tubes tucked inside his nose, and a blanket draped over his skeletal body, nicely turned down just under his chin. I lovingly watched as he slept. He looked peaceful.

At the moment, he felt no pain or worry about what was to come. I lay in my hospital bed and stared at the ceiling. Just a few months ago we were living our dream. We had great jobs, recently had our home built, and traveled frequently. We had plans... retire young, buy an RV, travel the country. Chad had plans... he had been working towards his administrator's license so he could become president of the company he worked for. Now our days were filled with hospitals, doctors, medications, and end-of-life decisions. Chad would not have the opportunity to live out his dreams or check off another item from his bucket list. As I rolled onto my side and looked at Chad, I thought life is not fucking fair!

My mom stayed at our house and drove back and forth to the hospital daily. Every morning she brought me clean clothes, and since Chad had a bathroom, I showered there. Chad's mom opted to stay at a hotel, since it was only two blocks away from the hospital.

The social worker, Cindi, checked on me daily. It was a struggle for her to get me to leave the room. I lived each day to make Chad's life memorable and comfortable. What if I wasn't there and he needed me? It was a fear that haunted me.

Cindi was a petite woman in her late fifties, soft spoken, and comfortable to talk to. She always encouraged me to walk outside with her to get some fresh air, and one day I finally agreed. I had no idea when I had last been outside and it felt good to feel sun on my face, with the smell of fresh cut grass in the air, and the sounds of cars, trucks, beeping horns. The hustle of people on the sidewalk. I didn't stay long; I was afraid. I didn't want Chad to be scared, and if I was with him he wouldn't be. Or that's what I thought. Plus, Chad was not able to leave the confines of his hospital room, so why should I be free to go outside? I immediately returned to his room.

Chad was brave, strong, courageous, in good spirits, never complained, never got mad, and never said, "Why me?" He never said it out loud anyway. He was extremely polite to everyone. When the nurse took his blood he said, "Thank you." When the nurse changed out his IV medications he said, "Thank you." When the nurse helped with his bedpan he said, "Thank you." When the nurse brought oral medication he said, "Thank you." When the nurse's aide changed his sheets, or filled the water pitcher he said, "Thank you." When the pain specialist left he said, "Thank you." When a visitor stopped by he said, "Thank you." As Dr. C left the room he said, "Thank you." He thanked my mom and his mom daily for spending time with him. Chad appreciated every person in his life, and always had.

It was mid-June and Chad could not stop talking about the annual family beach vacation. It ripped my heart out to see him want something so much, and to know that it would not happen. He was too weak and fatigued, and couldn't physically make the drive. But he desperately wanted to spend another week in Rehoboth Beach with me, his mom, his siblings and their significant others, and his nieces and nephews. I didn't want him to miss out and went in search of... something.

I scanned the internet on my phone and came across an app that played ocean sounds. When Chad slept, I turned on the ocean waves and tenderly placed my phone under his pillow. I hoped he had sweet dreams about being at the beach with his family.

As my husband lay dying in his hospital bed, I would sit at the end of his bed in a chair and a few times a day I would massage his swollen feet with peppermint lotion. It was something I could do to provide comfort for both of us. He said it felt good and he enjoyed it. For me, it was a way to lovingly touch my husband – maybe for the last time.

One afternoon, as I massaged Chad's left foot, I noticed several purple/bluish/red blotchy veins rising to the skin's surface on the soul of his foot. I quickly looked up the meaning on the internet, on my phone. These types of veins were due to reduced blood circulation, a sign that death was near, and was usually seen first on the bottom of the feet. I took a deep breath and looked up at Chad, but he had fallen asleep. As I continued to massage his left foot and stare at the purplish discoloration, I spotted a small red outline of an object, it was in the shape of a heart. I called my mom over.

"Look at this." I pointed to the tiny heart just below his third and fourth toes.

Our eyes sparkled with excitement. Chad was telling me that he loved me.

It was becoming more evident that the time was near. Chad wasn't eating or drinking. Sometimes he said he was hungry, but by the time we brought the food to him he didn't want it. I would continually brush his lips and the inside of his mouth with a wet swab. There were no more aware moments to share. Only faint words flowed from his lips, and his lifeless body lay still beneath the sheets.

Dying people often wait for someone or something, almost appearing as if they choose the moment to die. It was important to me that Chad knew he could leave us when he was ready. It was a Sunday, late morning, Chad's family was present, and we surrounded his bed as he slept. I caressed his left hand and his mom held his right hand, while everyone else joined hands in a circle. With tears streaming down my face, I started with a quote by Norman Cousins, "Love is stronger than death even though it can't stop death from happening, but no matter how hard death tries it can't separate people from love. It can't take away our memories either. In the end, love is stronger than death."

I could hardly get the words out, my deep love for Chad was almost unbearable. Chad's youngest nephew David was next. He thanked Chad for the fishing trips, the fossil digging, and being a great uncle. He ended with, "I'll see you in heaven in eighty years."

Lisa, Chad's sister was next... everyone took their turn and said what they felt was important for Chad to hear. It was extremely emotional for everyone. We all cried, some had to leave the room, and some said nothing; they just couldn't get the words out. None of us wanted Chad to hang on, waiting. I hoped we cleared the way for him to let go. Afterwards, there was a calm that engulfed my body. Deep in my soul, I knew it was time.

It was just after lunch on Wednesday and I could tell Chad was exhausted. His body was malnourished and dehydrated, and his health status was very poor. The cancer was devouring his body... it had consumed his liver, bones, and lungs. Over the last six months, I watched him go through too much pain and discomfort. I was prepared. I gathered my strength and walked to the hospital chapel with my mom by my side. From the hallway, I could see a beautiful stained glass window with a circular design that reminded me of the Circle of Life. As I entered the chapel, I looked around and took a seat in the back. I closed my eyes. My hands were clenched tightly together as I raised them to my chest. I bowed my head and prayed...

"Please God take him, I beg you to please end the pain and suffering today."

I opened my palms and laid my sobbing face in my hands. I slowly raised my body from the chair, but my head hung in shame, that I actually prayed for God to take him from us. How did I face Chad now, knowing I had prayed for his death?

Later that day my prayer was granted. Within hours after I left the chapel, a gurgling, congested sound projected from Chad's mouth. What was going on? I rushed to his bedside and stood and watched as I hovered over his struggling body. His eyes were closed, but could he see? See me? My mom and Chad's mom were by my side as I bobbed up and down on my knees, and under my breath repeated, "Please stop this God, please stop it now." I gently touched his left arm so he knew we were there, and my mom and Chad's mom did the same.

I bent over and whispered in his ear, "I love you, it's okay to let go."

We all quietly watched as he took his last breath and I waited... waited for another breath, but it never came. I screamed out "NO!" and fell across his lifeless body.

I sobbed hard and loud. At some point, I crawled into bed with him, wrapped my arms around him, and lay there for what felt like hours… but I knew it wasn't. I remembered his body cooling down in my arms. He was at peace now. I thanked God for answering my prayers. When I finally raised my head from Chad's chest and looked around the room, we were alone.

Chapter 6

NEXT TWENTY-FOUR HOURS

Once I walked away I would never see Chad's gray eyes, touch his tender hands, or kiss his soft lips again. Was I able to do this? It didn't matter, I had to. It wasn't a choice. I lay in bed next to Chad and stared as a nurse practitioner felt for a pulse and listened for his heartbeat. He was pronounced dead. She looked at me and offered her condolences; I just nodded... which expended the last drop of energy I had. A registered nurse Chad frequently had assigned to him on the evening shift said she would take good care of him. I cried and stuttered the words, "But he'll be alone."

"He will not be alone," she assured me.

Was she staying with him? Images flashed through my mind... his thin, pale, naked body lying on a table in the cold dark hospital basement, awaiting pick-up by the funeral home, or would his body be stored in a metal drawer, like I had seen on TV? Either way, he was alone. Would he have a sheet draped over him? An identification toe tag? I didn't want to leave Chad; I wanted one more night. My mom, Chad's mom, and Lynne said it was best if I went home. I didn't argue.

I don't recall leaving the hospital or the ride home, but I remember that my mom drove. She parked my car in the driveway next to Chad's car, the car he would never drive again. As I sat and stared at the front of our house, I flashed to escorting Chad out the front door three weeks earlier. Little did I know that was the beginning of our final journey together. As badly as I wanted to cry, I couldn't. My body had nothing left to give.

I swung open the front door of the house and a wave of emotion instantly rippled through my body. Our lives had been turned upside down, but there was no "our." It was only me now. I slowly walked down the hallway to our bedroom and collapsed on the bed. Mom lay next to me, and not a word was spoken. The excessive stress of the last six months had taken its toll. I was unable to feel, think, or even pick up my leg to cross over the other. Nothing runs on empty. I was asleep within minutes.

When I awoke the next morning, my mom was still in bed next to me. We talked softly about breakfast. She knew I needed to eat, but I had no appetite. I rolled over, placed my feet on the floor, and stood up. I was sore, like I was bruised all over my body, and the right side of my head throbbed. I hoped this was an awful nightmare, but I knew this was the start of my new life.

I looked around the bedroom. The IV pole was on Chad's side of the bed, his wallet and pocket change were on the top of his dresser, and his nightstand was filled with bottles of medication, a purple puke bag, and a dark green metal water bottle. I quickly tucked everything in a drawer and called hospice to pick up their equipment and supplies. The top of our bathroom counter still held Chad's blue toothbrush, which stuck out from its holder; his tube of toothpaste was to the right of the sink, and his electric razor was on the left. I immediately opened a vanity drawer and placed his things inside. If I didn't see his things, maybe I wouldn't have to feel the pain.

At times, I felt... relieved. Chad was set free of his suffering. I took comfort in knowing he was no longer in pain. But this feeling also brought me shame in that I felt I shouldn't feel this away about someone I love. My husband, the love of my life, the man I adored, was devoted to, and idolized. It was hard for me to process. How did I allow myself to feel comfort in his demise? I had to remind myself that Chad did not enjoy his suffering, and I did not enjoy watching. The turmoil, tough decisions, and exhaustion consumed both of our bodies in different ways, day after day after day. I have no regrets about what I was able to provide... I gave every second of my time, my full attention, and every ounce of my energy. I hoped it made a moment in his day a little easier. That's love. That's commitment. Until death do us part, which is what I promised. Chad's death was a welcome relief. I'm human.

There was one last thing I had to do for Chad. Celebrate his life.

Chapter 7

THE CELEBRATION OF CHAD'S LIFE

Memories of funerals from my childhood still haunt me.

My great grandmother was in her nineties when she passed. I was maybe ten. Her funeral was a social function... people shook hands, smiled, and chatted like they were at the local coffee shop. But there was one slight difference – her open casket was right there, in the same room with people chatting, like she was invisible. And this took place in her house!

It was my first funeral and one that terrified me, like a scary movie. I wanted to run home and jump in bed, pull the sheets over my head. My great grandmother laid in her house for three days and three nights. Every evening in front of the casket the preacher would turn the gospel into a screaming message, complete with spit spewing and froth bubbling from the corners of his mouth. With a powerful force the preacher yelled, "You are going to hell!"

My little mind froze and my eyes widened... what did he mean?

Then he howled something about "The fear of God."

I panicked. I had never experienced such a display of angry energy. Where was the kind, soft-spoken, and loving preacher? I burst into uncontrollable sobs. My dad put his arm around me, escorted me out of my great grandmother's house, and took me home. But this horrific memory is forever with me, and something I choose not to experience again.

Seven days after Chad's death, and with much help from family and friends, I hosted a celebratory event in honor of his life.

The lodge was a quiet and unique venue, with a cozy, rustic feel. The modern wood A-frame structure showcased an impressive staircase connecting the entry level to the lower level where the beautiful waterfront deck overlooked a pond and the serene, hilly countryside. Chad would love this place. It was perfect.

During the days immediately after Chad's death I focused on going through boxes of pictures and photo albums, carefully selecting an array from Chad's childhood through his more recent accomplishments and adventures. I also collected meaningful items: newspaper articles about him, a framed page from a magazine that told Chad's story about a fishing trip in the Pacific Northwest, and a few fishing flies he made. I was determined to let the guests into every aspect of my husband's accomplished life.

With the flurry of activity around planning this event, I continued to feel numb. Was my mind protecting me from the pain and the shock? Was it too much for me to process? Was it something my mind and body couldn't handle right now? I still felt as if I was walking through someone else's life, not mine.

As the guests entered the lodge, a small podium stood just inside. It held the guest book, a vase with two red roses that represented our love for each other, and an eight-by-ten framed photo of Chad kneeling in the Kapushka River on the Kamchatka Peninsula in Russia. In the picture, he's holding a large trout and has a huge smile on his face. This was reflective of a happy time, Chad enjoying his favorite sport of fishing. Chad was so excited when he and David decided to take this fishing trip six years earlier. The two of them would tell stories about dodging grizzly bears along the river, flying in a Russian military helicopter, and catching hundreds of fish. Chad had a deep appreciation for the outdoors and wildlife; he loved the tranquil feeling of it all. Fishing, no matter where, was the place he went to get away. This picture was not just the physical Chad, but it signified a lifetime of stories and memories. It's by far my favorite.

Chad's family and I greeted guests as they descended the staircase to the lower level. I was honored to be the first. It was hard to smile, but I did, slightly. In that moment of a shared handshake or hug, I represented not only myself, but also Chad. There was a sense of both honoring him, and showing respect. Seeing certain people triggered deep emotional responses, but I refrained from expressing them. I didn't want to be remembered as the hysterically grieving widow.

Father Lou was Chad's friend and confidante. He knew and understood Chad on a level that only he could. Father Lou assisted Chad through his most challenging problems and fears during his terminal illness. I was grateful for what he did, and what he meant to Chad. As Father Lou hugged me there was lump in my throat. I couldn't say a word. But he knew.

Chad had many success stories at work, but one always touched my heart because I knew she had a special place in Chad's heart. Lathea was a CNA (Certified Nursing Assistant) and could barely make ends meet as a single mother of three.

Chad had the vision and desire to help people who had aspirations but didn't know where and how to start. He designed a one-of-a-kind program that not only helped staff launch into a new and better paying career, but also to do it debt-free. She was his first success, and the beginning of many more. She loved Chad and had great respect and admiration for him. And he for her. I noticed her as she walked down the massive staircase; we locked eyes. I knew I would fall apart if I got closer, and I knew that she would do the same. We both had a deep connection, in different ways.

After greeting the family, the guests were directed to the four eight-foot tables that displayed the vast setup of Chad's short but remarkable life. The pictures began...

o   his grandmother holding him as a baby
o   on his first birthday with chocolate cake covering his smiling face
o   a young toddler in the saddle of large horse, while his father held him on
o   a towel wrapped around a young wet boy after a swim in the backyard pool
o   as an adolescent, holding creepy crawly things

The pictures gradually advanced in age...

o   his first car
o   his first wrestling match
o   high school football captain
o   attempting to rope a calf while riding a horse

Then college...

o   ROTC (Reserve Officers' Training Corps)
o   wrapped in bright orange cold-weather gear on a motorcycle in the winter time
o   college graduation with his parents
o   Chad commissioned as an officer in the U.S. Army

Moving on with his life...

- o a wedding photo
- o at karate class
- o his black belt certificate
- o in front of a class at work, lecturing
- o going to work in a silly costume because he lost a bet
- o dyed blond hair, for a "shave your head" fundraiser at work
- o a framed newspaper article about the one-of-a-kind nursing program he designed
- o Chad and Ernie Irving in front of his NASCAR

The last table was filled with various pictures of Chad around the world – Russia, South Africa, Aruba, South Carolina, Washington State, Florida, Missouri, Alaska, Bahamas, and Mexico. At the end was a large glass vase filled with bite-size Snickers candies. A small frame sat next to the vase, "This was Chad's favorite candy, please help yourself."

By focusing the event on Chad's pleasures, accomplishments, and adventures throughout his life, it prompted the sharing of stories and discussions of him in a positive way. I wanted people to remember Chad when they picked up a Snickers bar, or they heard someone talk about fishing, or something else that caught their attention. I was proud of the display, and grateful to my family for their help and love. I could have never done this alone.

Even though the day focused on celebrating Chad's life, it was immensely draining physically for me, and what little emotion I had was gone. At the end of it all, I crawled into bed. My stomach growled and I wasn't sure if I had eaten all day. But the thought of putting anything in my mouth made me nauseous. I just wanted to go to sleep and wake up in the past, with Chad.

Chapter 8

THE NEXT FEW WEEKS

My mom had spent five weeks with us, and an additional two weeks after the memorial service with me. She needed to go home, but I didn't want to be alone. What would it be like to be alone?

The thought of it terrified me, like the dream I had over and over as a child. My dad was driving our family's large 1960 Chevy while I stood on the hump in the back floorboard, my small arms draped over the middle of the bench seat in front of me. Dad and I were having fun on our evening cruise. At some point, he turned the car onto a dark tree-lined road – no houses, no street lights, and no other cars. After a few minutes of driving into infinite darkness, he pulled over to the side of the road and parked in a large gravel lot. Dad maneuvered the car so the headlights partially lit up an area that headed towards the densely wooded tree line. He turned to me and said, "You be good, and stay in the car."

He opened the car door, got out, and closed the door behind him. I stared as my dad walked in the illuminated space, towards the trees. He entered the wooded area and never looked back at me. I waited and waited, straining my eyes for his silhouette to appear, but it never did. I was alone in a dark place that was unfamiliar. Every time I had that dream as a child, I awakened more horrified than the last time. Sometimes I would lay in bed and scream at the top of my lungs for my mom.

During the day, thoughts would flash through my mind. As I folded laundry, I wondered why Chad didn't have any clothes in this load, wondered what he would like for dinner. My cell phone would ring... maybe it was Chad. When I looked at the clock in the evening I'd think Chad should be home from work soon. I wished this were all true. I craved his touch, kiss, his voice, to hold his hand.

The capacity or the desire to concentrate on anything for long periods of time was nonexistent. The wave of emotions and the inability to get much rest because I cried myself to sleep most nights, led me to a decision. Consciously I couldn't allow myself to get paid for a job I could not competently perform, so I resigned. It felt good. Was I beginning to think about myself?

I didn't huddle up in a ball and feel sorry for myself, nor was I bored. It seemed like everything I did was in slow motion, as if my mind needed more time than normal to process a task. Or was it my body needing to conserve the already low energy level? What I could do was focus and exert energy for short periods of time – run the vacuum, wash a few dishes, open mail, make a phone call, fix myself a bowl of cereal. The pain and grief were still unbearable at times, but I tried to stay occupied, sending out death certificates to life insurance companies, notifying banks, credit unions, mortgage companies, and investment firms of Chad's death. Hundreds of thank-you cards. I did the best I could, which sometimes wasn't much.

I strategically planned my day. I didn't go shopping during peak hours, I did my banking in the bank drive-thru, I walked through the park during a time of day when everyone else was at work. I intentionally dodged people because I dreaded the question, "How are you doing?"

I always replied, "I'm okay," which meant not good, but not bad.

I didn't want to drag anyone down with my hard moments. Plus, people didn't need to hear the truth and I didn't want to relive it again. My fear was that if I permitted myself to wallow too much in the heartbreak, I would get stuck there forever. My perspective was not a pleasant place to spend time.

Friends stopped by occasionally and family members called daily. Each would say, "Take care of yourself."

"I am," I would always reply.

But I wasn't sure what that meant anymore. I took care of what I had to… eating, showering, and paying bills. I used to think if you ate right, exercised, and lived a healthy lifestyle you'd be around until you were old and gray. It wasn't true. But there was hope in imagining that if I lived in a healthy way my body would have the ability to fight off anything. In reality, it was just a belief that didn't allow my mind to run away with thoughts of my own mortality.

Nighttime continued to be a battle with frightening outcomes, one in particular. I was awakened in the middle of the night by my jolting body. My heart pounded hard against my chest wall. I couldn't catch my breath and was drenched in sweat, frozen with fear. Three large men dressed in black yelled and screamed as they waved their guns, but I couldn't remember what they said. Chad and I sat in metal chairs with our hands tied behind our backs, and our legs tied together, with our feet on the floor. We attempted to negotiate with our captors, but to no avail. In the end, one of them placed the barrel of his large black handgun against the base of

Chad's head and pulled the trigger. His head collapsed towards his chest. I screamed as I helplessly watched my husband die yet another tragic death. As I trembled with fear, I couldn't help but wonder what that all meant?

Some dreams were beautiful and comforting... Chad and I made passionate love in our bed. Did he know about the awful dream from the night before? Did he reach down to comfort me the only way he could? When I awoke the next morning, there was a newfound calmness. I imagined his long, strong arms wrapped around me and felt safe.

Some mornings I lay in bed and remember... Chad had an innocent ability to annoy me. Every weekday morning his alarm clock would sound off at 6:00 a.m., sometimes earlier, with a high-pitched beep, beep, beep! I would jab him gently with an elbow, and he would roll over and hit the snooze button. This would continue most mornings for an entire hour. After the third round of beep, beep, beeps, I was wide awake. I tried to explain, "If you set your clock for one hour later, you could get additional restful sleep."

His response: "I need to get up earlier than that."

I would just scratch my head. I longed for that annoyance now.

The last seven months expended every drop of my emotional energy. Everything inside me was empty and I felt isolated, but some of the isolation was my own doing. I needed to break the cycle and give myself permission to enjoy, laugh, do something fun, and not feel guilty for a moment of happiness.

It took a few weeks, but I finally took the advice of a widow friend, an aesthetician. She invited me to her spa for a facial treatment. As I lay flat on my back on her table – mud on my face, a mask over my eyes, and hands and feet wrapped in warm towels – my mind went blank and my body drooped in relaxation. As I concentrated on my inhalation/exhalation, a vision slowly came to life: Chad was sitting quietly on a mountaintop with his knees drawn into his chest, the sun partially hidden behind the mountain range in the distance. Chad had his back to me and appeared as if he were watching the sunset. Animals surrounded him... hopping rabbits, darting squirrels, birds swooping, butterflies fluttering nearby, and two deer standing motionless to his right. I begged him to turn around so I could see his face, but he never did. The vision left as quickly as it came but I felt as if Chad was telling me he was okay and at peace. A single tear trickled out of the corner of each eye and a level of tranquility filled every fiber of my being. I grinned with pleasure.

Later that evening I thought about the fact that whenever Chad and I could, mostly when we were on vacation, we took the time to watch the sunset. We would hold hands and walk along the white sand beach, or find a beachfront bar and watch the sun disappear on the horizon. Words were rarely spoken as we absorbed the beauty and the energy. In some way, I felt connected to a deeper part of my soul. I was thankful for being with the one I loved and grateful to be alive to experience such splendor. I was happy to see Chad continue our romantic ritual.

Everything was different. Meals alone, a different routine... what did my future hold? All these changes made me feel cut off and disconnected from my life, or what my life had been. I woke up in the morning and went to bed at night alone. There was no noise in the house, only the sounds I made. I had conversations with myself. And playing the air guitar in my pajamas to a classic rock song, with no one else there, just didn't have the same effect. I lived a life of existence, or was it survival?

I had to "accept" the abrupt finality of death. There was nothing I could do to bring Chad back. Eventually, my life would change again. That's the way life happens. I had to willingly accept it. There was no other choice.

Chapter 9

WHAT WAS NEXT?

As I looked around the house there were so many reminders.

Chad's favorite recliner loveseat, a pair of his shoes tucked under the bench in the mudroom, wooden end tables he had made, the valances we hung together in both the sunroom and our bedroom. Four years earlier I had asked Chad to go to the furniture store with me; he furrowed his brow but agreed. As I showed him the two nightstands I wanted, his attention was drawn to the intricately patterned alder, cherry, and white ash burl dresser. He opened the drawers to admire the fine craftsmanship of the joints and then lifted his head, looked at me, and grinned. I knew that look. What started as two nightstands ended with an additional six-foot dresser with a matching mirror, and a four-drawer chest with a marble top. It was delivered to our house a few days later. The large dresser was now filled with Chad's t-shirts, workout clothes, socks, polo shirts, underwear, shorts, swim trunks, and a small junk drawer. He had a certain way he organized, folded, and stored his clothes.

On the top of Chad's dresser sat a beautifully polished wooden box. To the right was a framed picture of the two of us at sunset, sitting on white sand in Myrtle Beach, South Carolina. On the left side was the last picture we had taken together, snowshoeing only days before I whisked him off to the emergency room.

As I opened the hinged top of the wooden box, Chad's smiling face appeared. Tucked inside the lid was my favorite picture of him holding a trout in the Kapushka River, the same picture from his memorial service. A removable tray underneath the lid was filled with Chad's military ID card, New York State Driver's License, military coins, and foreign currency. Below the tray was the box that held Chad's ashes. I could not grasp the fact that his incinerated body was in this box. Every time I looked at it my stomach tightened and tears rolled down my face. I imagined Chad's chauffeured body in a hearse, on the way to the crematorium, on July 4th. Why did I notice the date on the certificate, it served no actual purpose. But will I always remember his ride on this publicly celebrated holiday?

As I opened Chad's closet doors, I saw that the top rack was filled with a colorful array of long-sleeved collared shirts for work, and pushed to the right were a few fleece zip-up jackets. On the lower rack were hangers of Levi's, khakis, dress slacks, and two overflowing tie racks. Chad wore a tie to work most days and had one for every occasion and holiday, even the Fourth of July.

I had an intimate connection with every piece of Chad's clothing; I couldn't allow just anyone to have his clothes. Donating them was out of the question. What if I saw a stranger in one of Chad's shirts? I wasn't sure how I would react to that, and I didn't want to find out. What could I do that would have a meaningful outcome for me and the people that loved Chad?

As I scanned his clothes I saw a few things that held special meaning: the red knit hat Chad wore on his bald head, and the "Cancer Sucks" t-shirt. After sorting through all his t-shirts, I realized that I couldn't let go of any of them. Not a single one. Chad wore a t-shirt every evening at home, on the weekends, and while he worked around the house. Each one I touched reminded me of fun times... the Memorial Day run we did together, the Corporate Challenge we did together, the American Red Cross Blood Donation we did together. How could I ever let go of these? Then there was the yellow zip-up fleece that Chad wore often, which was a favorite of mine too. When I would wrap something around my body on cool evenings, it wasn't a blanket or a quilt, it was this fleece of Chad's.

I continued to see my grief therapist every other Tuesday. Losing Chad was no doubt one of my life's most painful experiences. The tornado of emotion that ripped through my body did just that, ripped up my insides leaving me with headaches, tight muscles, and digestive issues from the worry and anxiety. My response was similar during the months my father struggled prior to his death, and the abrupt death of my father-in-law. But talking to Cindi about death, about difficult people in my life, about my not working or making a contribution to society, about how unfair life was... it helped me get it out of my ripped-up body, which so needed to be repaired.

Time. Give yourself time, she would say. "And permission, give yourself permission to feel bad, to cry, to scream, to feel good, to laugh... don't deny yourself."

At the start of most sessions I was actually smiling; Cindi brought that out in me with her uplifting comments and empathy. She always made the right statement at the right time. Or sometimes, she would just listen and not say a word. That helped too. By the end of many sessions I would have used several tissues. Crying was okay, too.

Nancy, a friend of ours who lived down the street, was an amazing quilt designer and maker. She had won numerous awards. I called her and described my plan for Chad's shirts and asked her to stop by when she had a chance. Nancy came by later that afternoon and I escorted her to our bedroom and opened Chad's closet. She looked at the shirts and felt the fabric and said that she was positive we could make quilts for my nieces and nephews.

The thought of turning Chad's shirts into treasured gifts was exciting to me. For the next several weeks I hauled bags of shirts to Nancy's house and spent hours cutting ten-inch squares from the front and back of every shirt. We designed each individual quilt based on gender. The girls' quilts were made of pink, purple, and more feminine colors, while the boys' were made of blues, green, and strong deep colors.

Nancy carefully stitched each quilt and backed it with fabric I selected, characteristic of each child. Each one was finished off with an embroidered square of fabric sewn on the back that included their name and the words, "Uncle Chad is watching over you." The quilts were beautiful, and a perfect gift, something they could sleep with, cover up with on a chilly day, or hang on their wall. Nancy decided there were enough squares to make a big quilt for me. I was thrilled. Every time I look at that quilt I remember each shirt and the tie he wore with it. I remember my favorites.

Chad's boat was still in storage, and with fall approaching it would soon be a new storage season. I knew I would never use the boat, and paying for another year of storage seemed ridiculous. Chad's vehicle had a tow hitch; I could pick up the boat, clean it up, and put it on Craigslist. I had never towed anything in my life, but I would learn quickly.

The boat, or "Mothra" as Chad called her, had been a part of our lives longer than we were married. He bought Mothra at a Boat Show in Seattle when we were both stationed in the U.S. Army at Fort Lewis. She had been in the

Pacific Ocean, on many lakes, and was towed across the country when we moved to Syracuse. It was a tough decision, but I needed to let her go to a new home where she would be used and enjoyed.

When I called the storage facility owner, Ken, also a friend, he said he would bring the boat anywhere I wanted it dropped. I never expected that! It was a generous offer by a considerate and thoughtful man. He didn't want payment in return; he did it out of the kindness of his heart. I was grateful for the many wonderful people in my life, but I also had one that was not so nice.

About two months after Chad's death, someone who defined herself as a friend called and asked me to dinner. I was surprised by her invitation, because she rarely supported us when times were good, and when Chad got sick she never called, texted, or offered to help in any way. Worse yet, she never visited him in the hospital. But that night at dinner she spewed the most insensitive garbage I'd ever heard. How excited she was that Chad was no longer around and she now had the opportunity to become number one in her husband's life. I only sat and listened out of respect for the relationship between Chad and her husband. I have not seen or talked to her since that vicious night. Over time, I was able to forgive her, but I did so for me, not for her.

The pain and grief were still unbearable, at times. Although friends and family called or texted daily, there were times I felt utterly alone and hollow. Sometimes I thought about how Chad had suffered and struggled with his deteriorating body and it made my heart ache that he experienced such a harsh fight. I missed him every single day... his laugh, lying next to him, and hearing him walk down the hall. This just wasn't fair.

To give me support as only Chad could, I combed the internet for an item I could put some of his ashes in. I wanted to carry Chad with me on walks or hiking adventures, those planned trips that would not happen together. Plus, he gave me strength and confidence to do things I wasn't sure of. It turned out there were many websites that had hundreds of items: rings, pendants, lockets, bracelets. What caught my eye was a silver heart pendent with a small Mother-of-Pearl heart on the upper right lobe, and wings molded into the front. It was a peaceful piece, and the heart shape was representative of our love. When it arrived in the mail I could not fathom placing the ashes into the heart – I just couldn't do it. I called the funeral director and asked if he would do that for me, and he graciously agreed.

I waited outside on the front porch of the funeral home while inside he opened the box, the bag, and removed ashes to place in the pendant. I couldn't think about it. He returned the box and the charm. I immediately put on the necklace, and wore it for months without taking it off. To this day, when I wear it, I find that I sometimes unconsciously touch it when I'm in an uneasy situation.

Chad's birthday was fast approaching. He would have been forty-six. Chocolate cake with chocolate icing was his favorite, and every year I made him one. One year I attempted to make a healthier cake, low-fat, and he immediately recognized the difference. Every year thereafter Chad would request a "regular full-fat" cake. But there would be no cake and no celebratory dinner with friends this year, or any other year. However, I could not allow his birthday to go unrecognized.

The park that Chad and I frequented many evenings after dinner had wooden benches under a tree, along a trail, and near the canal waterway. Each of them had a plaque attached in memory of someone. Our evening walks were fun... we held hands, talked, and watched the fish, birds, turtles, and occasionally a snake.

Chad would sometimes pull his hand away from mine and say, "Don't hold my hand, people will think we're together." Then he'd laugh.

He loved to kayak down the canal while throwing his fishing line in the water, or fishing from the top of the aqueduct.

I approached the volunteer park manager one day and asked about the benches.

"Sure, you can buy one," he said.

I ordered it on the spot and gave my request for its placement – near the aqueduct. A few weeks later the bench was in place, a beautiful bronze plaque with Chad's name was attached to the seat back, and flowers already lay on the bench. Someone else missed Chad too.

My birthday was two months after Chad's, and it would be my fiftieth. He had agreed to take me to Hawaii, but that wasn't going to happen. Ten years earlier my sister-in-law Cathy and I had gone to Hawaii to run a half marathon; it was our first visit to the islands, and our first marathon. After one week in paradise I called Chad and told him to pack up everything, we were moving.

He laughed and said, "When will you be home?"

I loved Hawaii... the culture, the weather, the people, and their belief in togetherness. After mulling it over for a few days I thought, "Why couldn't I go?"

I called my travel agent and asked her to book it. I was going to Hawaii... alone.

Chapter 10

MY 40TH BIRTHDAY

He forgot, but not really.

Ten years earlier, it had been just like any other morning. We watched the news in bed, showered, and discussed our evening plans while we got ready for work. Chad had a busy day ahead and a board meeting at 5:00 p.m. He gave me a kiss and said, "Have a good day, I'll be home late," and he left the house.

I drove to work a little disappointed that he had not wished me Happy Birthday, but the day wasn't over yet. The minutes and hours ticked by, nothing from Chad. By the end of the day, I was upset and felt forgotten by my husband. I was hurt. On my drive home, I stopped and picked up take-out. It was my birthday and I wanted a treat, no cooking.

The phone rang several times as I ate dinner alone in the dining room. My brother, my mom, and many friends called to express their birthday wishes. At this point I knew Chad was in his board meeting and I wouldn't hear from him until he arrived home. He had never done this before and my emotions led me to a pity party. I knew he loved me and he didn't do this on purpose, but it still hurt. Around 10:00 p.m. I heard a car pull up and the dog barked. Chad opened the front door and walked towards the bedroom, where I was watching television in bed. He looked into my teary eyes and said, "What's up?"

I quietly stared into his eyes for what felt like several minutes. He stared back and finally lifted his left arm and twisted his wrist to view his watch. It was like a light bulb went off, and he said, "Oh my God, I'm so sorry. I forgot your birthday."

He sat down on the edge of the bed and gave me a big kiss. I smiled. That kiss made up for so much. I was one happy wife.

Three months earlier Chad had informed me that he wanted to buy me a muscle car for my upcoming birthday. I was ecstatic! I had been a motorhead since high school and loved old, loud, fast cars. Over the next few weeks I bought car magazines and searched the internet. Nothing.

Chad called his Uncle Kip, another motorhead, who happened to be headed to a car show in Pennsylvania. Chad explained to Kip what we were looking for and within two hours Kip called back. He found a really nice car, and it was for sale. We drove the few hours south to check out the car – a blue metallic 1969 Chevy Chevelle, two-door, bucket seats, rally wheels, 350 engine that produced over 300 horsepower, a Sun Super Tachometer, and Dynomax headers. It was just what I was looking for and we bought it on the spot.

I felt like a princess with a diamond crown. This car was something I had always wanted but thought I'd never own. Chad rarely drove the car, always saying, "It's your car."

We attended car shows, car parties, and just cruised around town. I never liked the front license attached to the front bumper of a muscle car, not sure why. So, my front plate was always displayed on the front dashboard. The many times I tromped on the gas and got squirrely, the plate would freely fly around the inside of the car and ricochet off the windows and roof. Chad would say in a serious voice, "Would you please let me know before you do that? I need to duck or put my hands on that plate before one of us gets hurt."

He would then go on to say, "Actually, lets attach the plate on the front of the car, where it is supposed to be."

My reply, "No way."

We enjoyed the car together for two months before we had to put her in storage for the winter. I loved that car and we had so much fun with her. So, when Chad forgot my birthday, he really didn't. He put forth a huge effort in finding and purchasing this outrageous gift, and I was thankful. After thinking about my wonderful present, I felt a little ridiculous about being upset. I was emotional because he was caught up in a busy work day and a board meeting, and all I wanted to hear was Happy Birthday! Words I will never hear from him again.

Chapter 11

MY 50TH BIRTHDAY

It was almost six months since Chad passed away.

My days were becoming a little easier, because my mind had accepted the fact that Chad was gone. He was not on an adventure across the globe and would not be returning with funny stories and hundreds of pictures to share. Life was full of changes.

Almost two years earlier Chad and I traveled to Aruba on our last tropical vacation together. Chad had never enjoyed the flying experience.

He always said, "I feel like herded cattle."

As I boarded the plane alone in Syracuse on a cold December morning, I thought about the herded cattle. I grinned and giggled under my breath. It was kind of true. I had a window seat, with a stranger seated next to me. There would be no sharing a movie, splitting a peanut butter and banana sandwich (which I always took when we flew), no discussion on what vacation activities we were interested in, and no leaning my head on the shoulder next to me. I couldn't help but lunge forward, and wonder, what was this trip to Hawaii really going to be like?

After short layovers in Detroit and Los Angeles, but many hours in the air, the plane was on its final approach to Kona... on the Big Island of Hawaii. As the plane banked to the left and turned towards the runway, I could see the immense black lava fields that surrounded the airport. When the plane landed, chatter erupted; everyone was excited about their vacation.

The plane door opened and I eagerly watched as the rows in front of me debarked. I grabbed my backpack, entered the aisle, and said thank you to the flight crew as I stepped off the plane and onto a mobile ramp.

A breeze of warm fresh air brushed across my face and I inhaled deeply as I continued down the ramp, where it met the tarmac. I followed the people in front of me as they headed towards the gate at this unique airport – no jet ways, no walls, no roof, open air – traditional Hawaiian style, and built on the 1801 lava flow from Hualalai volcano.

It was a short walk to baggage claim and a quarter mile shuttle ride to the car rental. I was tired, and I had a peculiar nervous feeling. Was it because I was alone? Or because I was uncertain that this was the right thing to do? Or because it was my first trip alone after Chad's death? Or maybe because it brought me pleasure and that made me uncomfortable. It may have been all of the above.

My birthday was two days away and I relaxed on the beach, toured Kailua-Kona village, and adjusted to the five-hour time difference. As I sat on my oceanfront lanai and enjoyed the palm trees swaying against the bright orange sunset, I reflected.

This moment reminded me of the precious sunsets with Chad. I placed my right hand on the heart pendant that rested on my chest. Chad was here with me, not in the physical sense, but he would always be in my heart and soul. With my focus on the consistent sound of the waves rolling onto the beach, calmness slowly moved from my head down to my toes. This was my new therapy space to ponder, reflect, make decisions, and just relax. Just because something terrible had happened, it didn't mean I couldn't embrace life and take the opportunities presented. Chad would have wanted that.

It was December 19th, my fiftieth birthday, and I woke up to many text messages. It was an amazing feeling to have so many thoughtful friends and a loving family. For a few minutes I felt fulfilled, but I quickly fell into a hollow state. This was just another first of not having Chad present.

Christmas was only a few days away, and then New Year's, which would be the one-year mark of the dreaded emergency room visit and hospitalization, with a diagnosis just days later. My birthday wish had always been to have an enjoyable dinner with Chad and close friends, and this year was no exception. Although I never imagined I would be celebrating by myself. Looking back at that now, it seems so petty. Maybe I should have thought out my birthday wish a little better... Chad and I together until we were one hundred years old. If I could only go back, would it have made a difference?

Upon arriving in Kona, I had called and made a birthday dinner reservation for sunset at the Beach Tree at the Four Seasons Hualalai. The restaurant was open air; it overlooked a gorgeous white sand beach with a breathtakingly beautiful blue ocean view. I sat alone at a table for two, and admired the scenery as the bright sun dipped into the ocean.

I flashed to my birthday celebration the year before. It was a typical snowy December evening in Syracuse. Chad had prearranged two of my best friends and their spouses to join us for dinner at our favorite restaurant: Daniella's Steakhouse. Not long after we were seated, Charlie, the owner, announced to the entire restaurant that it was my birthday. Cheers broke out and I wanted to crawl under the table from embarrassment. How did I get from there to here, thousands of miles away and alone? I lowered my head into my Kindle to keep my mind occupied. But that didn't work for long; I suddenly became anxious and the tears rolled. I buried my face deeper into my Kindle where no one would see me. I could not bear sitting there alone. Was anyone else alone at this romantic resort? But why did it matter at that moment? Eventually I pulled it together enough to order food and drink. I sat in silence as I read.

According to Merriam Webster, the word birthday is defined as the day when someone was born or the anniversary of that day. I know December 19 was the day I was born, but this year, was it the day I would redefine my purpose? Since my life had been turned upside down, I felt the desire to ponder the reason for existence. Everything has a purpose, and I was forced into change. To find new meaning and a new way of life.

Chapter 12

HAWAII

My first run on a beautiful Kona morning was along the coast on Alii Drive, towards the village of Kailua-Kona.

The sun was bright against the glorious blue sky, and at one point I stopped to gaze at the white-capped waves as they rolled onto the curvy coastline. A large wave crashed into a nearby black lava rock floodwall, which created a loud "boom," as the ground gently shook below me. When I reached the village, I admired the array of shops and restaurants that lined both sides of the street. I continued down the sidewalk where I eventually crossed over a metal gate and onto the pedestrian-only pier, and walked to the end, where I turned around and appreciated the view from the water: Hualalai (one of five volcanoes on the island, now inactive), and a church steeple against the cloudless sky.

Mokauikaua Church was a large stone structure, and the oldest church in Hawaii. Its steeple towered over the village and had served as a navigational aid for almost two centuries.

As I pulled out my phone to take a picture, I noticed a gentleman about my age who struggled to walk with a cane. He approached me and I said, "Hi, how are you today?"

He replied in an upbeat voice and with a smile, "I'm doing great today, thanks."

Part of me was sad for him, and the other part felt pure admiration. In his mind, he was great, and that was all that mattered. That moment made me even more aware that I had a lot to be thankful for.

As I returned to my condo complex after my run I noticed a young woman at the concierge desk. I walked over and asked her about things to do on the island and she marked up a colorful paper map with several popular sites and handed it to me. In a soft, friendly voice, she asked, "Who are you traveling with?" I froze. My voice could not escape my throat. What would I say? I didn't want people to know I was traveling alone. I finally squeaked out, "Me, myself, and I."

She continued to probe in a friendly manner, "You're not married, or a boyfriend, a friend, family?"

My throat tightened as the anxiety set in. She fired one question after the other. "How long are you here? What are your plans?"

I didn't blink once, but caught myself holding my breath. I picked up a bottle of cold water from the several she had on her desk, twisted the top off, and took a large gulp. Her eyes continued to focus on me. "Where are you from? What do you do? You are really in paradise alone?"

We stared into each other's eyes, and then came a long pause... she expected answers. I felt trapped in a corner with no way out. I nervously blurted out, "I lost my husband six months ago, and yes I'm alone."

Her face immediately dropped and she replied, "I'm so sorry."

We stared into each other's tear-filled eyes as she stretched out both arms and wrapped them around me. I welcomed her embrace, although a sense of uneasiness washed over me. It was the same feeling I got as a kid when I hid a secret and someone pressured me to reveal it. But this time, I had attempted to protect my truth, my secret. I was not emotionally ready to open my deepest wounds to a stranger and not sure I would ever be ready.

The next several days were spent visiting some of the local tourist spots the concierge marked on my map. It was almost a daily occurrence to see green sea turtles on the beach. They were amazing to watch, almost like a slow-motion movie. I especially enjoyed watching them gracefully swim out into the ocean. They would get caught on top of a powerful wave and somehow manage to not get forced against the lava rock, which could crush them. It was as if they had a sense of the danger around them, and they maneuvered away from the threat.

One afternoon I watched a turtle for over one hour as it slowly crawled up the sandy beach to sunbathe and sleep. Within minutes of settling in, a huge wave crashed in and pulled it back into the ocean. Eventually, I saw the turtle floating in a wave. It appeared to struggle, but with determination, it finally caught the right wave, which gently placed it back on the sand, and it crawled up the beach once again.

According to Hawaiian history, the honu (sea turtle) symbolizes longevity, safety, and spiritual energy, and is also considered to be a bearer of good luck and peace. Native Hawaiians also believe the honu acts as their spiritual guide, protecting and leading them through life. Was this my spiritual guide? Then it hit me. I gained confidence and strength from watching these creatures struggle for their lives, but with patience and time they reached their goal.

Prior to Chad's death, we had briefly discussed our interests in various Hawaiian adventures. We both loved to hike, and his passion was fishing. So, I decided to do some of the adventures we discussed, to honor him and our plans.

The Hawaii Volcanoes National Park, located on the east side of the island, was a "Chad adventure." The volunteers at the Visitors' Center recommended hiking the Kīluaea Iki Trail, which was a four-mile moderate to challenging hike that would take two to three hours. I accepted the challenge, bought a guidebook, and drove the two miles to the trailhead.

My backpack was loaded with bottled water, protein bars, and almonds, as I started the hike around the crater rim. I descended four hundred feet through the rain forest, which was cool and shady, and then dropped down to the extremely hot uneven crater floor. The still-steaming floor was the actual surface of the lava lake that flooded Kīluaea Iki in 1959, and the thought of the two-mile hike to the other side was quite daunting, but there were ahu (rock cairns) that marked the way.

It was a crystal-clear day. With the sun blazing down on me, I slowly walked and stopped at each trail sign to read the story in the guidebook that matched the marker of the dramatic eruption all those years ago. It was an incredible educational experience and one Chad would have loved. I took comfort in the heart pendant that was around my neck, but felt intense sadness that Chad would never have this experience. The guilt was like a boulder on my heart.

Another Chad adventure was to Mauna Kea Volcano at almost fourteen thousand feet above sea level. I arrived at the visitor's center, which was located at eight thousand feet, around noon. I had lunch while I acclimated to the higher elevation. Kona was a balmy eighty-five degrees when I left, and an hour later I was sitting in a cool, breezy, forty-eight degrees. I wondered what the wind chill was?

The park ranger gathered everyone who was heading to the summit and gave a brief lecture. We then watched a short movie that described elevation sickness and how to handle it, and provided the history of this sacred land. After the movie, the caravan of ten vehicles, led by the park ranger, drove very slowly up the mountain to the summit for the next eight miles and parked outside Keck Observatory. As I swung open the car door, the brisk air brushed across my face and I thought I was going to freeze in place. After the initial shock of the wind chill, I followed the group into the building, where the tour began.

The observatory housed the largest optical and infrared twin telescopes in the world, each standing eight stories high. Astronomers from all around the globe used them to study the local and distant universe. When the enormous roof of the observatory opened slightly and the eighty-foot telescope moved in a circular motion, it felt unreal, like I was an extra in a science fiction movie.

After a brief discussion on how the telescope operated, we were dismissed to the cold weather elements. The sun was beginning to descend and this was the biggest reason I came to the summit, to watch the sun set. As I stood in the freezing temperatures, my body shivered from head to toe, and I noticed there were no trees or plants – the surface of the summit looked dead and even had an eerie feel. But maybe that feeling was the side effect of the thinner air and decreased mental and physical alertness.

As the sun dropped through the sky, it created an amazing variation of orange colors as it moved in and out of the clouds. And the reflection of the sun bounced a beam of light downward, across the sky. This was the most dramatic sunset I had ever seen. As I experienced this breathtaking moment, I felt a close connection drawing me towards the heavens. I felt almost weightless as I stared across the sky. As I enjoyed the peacefulness this space brought, I felt a quick but powerful sensation that shot through my entire body, head to toe. Was it God who touched me, or reached out to me? Was it Chad? Was it a force from another world? As the sun disappeared, I stood there in disbelief – what did I just experience?

The Big Island of Hawaii offered some of the best sport fishing in the world. Chad's love for fishing led me to charter an entire boat for myself. When I pulled into the harbor early that morning it was still dark. The only lights were those of the fishing boats preparing to head out into the open water. I found Captain Jeff's slip, parked the car, and grabbed my large tote bag filled with food, water, and a change of clothes.

Jeff welcomed me aboard and introduced me to his deckhand, Mike. I took a seat and closely watched as they set up the boat for a day of fishing. Mike placed reels on the rods, put the rods in holders, and organized the lures and fishing line. It was still dark as Jeff pulled away from the slip and slowly motored through the harbor, and within a few minutes we were out in the open water. Mike gave me specific instructions on what to do if a fish took the bait. The chair was daunting – I had to strap myself in so the fish couldn't take me overboard, and I had to place the mammoth rod in a holder between my legs. After this was accomplished, I had to crank on the reel to get the fish closer to the boat. Depending on the size of a particular fish, and its will to fight, it could take hours.

As nervous as I was about catching a fish, I somehow relaxed while staring at the calm ocean. The sun rose over the mountains just as quickly as it descended into the horizon at sunset. The colors were a little different, not as vibrant, maybe because there was a haze across the top of the mountains. It was a glorious sunrise, but I didn't enjoy it as much as the sunsets. Perhaps this was due to the shared fondness Chad and I had for them. I desperately missed those moments with him.

After six hours of fishing, we had no action and Mike began to wind down the fishing equipment while Jeff headed towards the harbor. It was a beautiful, relaxing day on the water and I felt a sense of satisfaction; I had honored Chad and one of his pleasures.

The village of Kailua-Kona displayed a few holiday lights and a decorated tree, nothing extravagant like you'd find on the mainland, but we did have a Christmas parade. With the warm weather and palm trees, it didn't feel like the holiday was near. I imagined my friends and family back east... drinking wine, watching the flames dance in the fireplace, and snow gently accumulating on the ground. I missed them, particularly the celebration of my birthday and now Christmas. But I chose to be alone; it was best for me. No tree to buy or decorations to haul up from the basement; it was too much to think about, let alone physically do. I didn't want to feel obligated to make an appearance at friends' or family's homes, and drum up the fake social energy, complete with a smile. I had no plans and no expectations for the day; it would be what it was. But I did think about what Chad would want me to be doing. This was easy. He wouldn't want me to have a horrible day.

I found a quaint open-air bar, poolside, and became friendly with the bartender, Diane. She was in her early fifties with a big smile and short blond hair. She was witty and somewhat comical, and she enjoyed introducing everyone at the bar to create one collective group. Diane explained to me how she flew from Pennsylvania to Hawaii thirty-five years earlier on vacation, and did not return. We swapped stories like we were sisters and a bond formed, although I did not divulge my secret truth.

On Christmas Eve, I felt a bit lonely and found Diane working at the bar. I asked her what she was doing for Christmas and she told me about her "Ohana," her Hawaiian family, and how they celebrate each year. She was responsible for her traditional cake, and she needed a few ingredients, but was concerned that the grocery store would be closed by the time she got off work. I told her I was going out for dinner, and to make a list. I'd pick up her groceries.

The bar was much busier when I returned later that evening. I quietly placed a small brown paper bag at the end of the bar and ordered a drink. Diane eventually slowed down enough to notice the bag, and she looked inside. Her eyes widened and a bright big smile lit up her face. She scanned the bar, her eyes locked on mine, and she asked me what she owed me and I said, "Nothing, Merry Christmas!" Diane's smile got even bigger and she turned and announced to everyone that I had made her day. I felt like Santa Claus. One small gesture brightened my day, and made her day a little easier. Wasn't that what Christmas was about?

A few days later I saw Diane and she presented me with a book: *Practice Aloha, Secrets to Living Life Hawaiian Style*. On the inside cover she wrote, "For Leah, who always practices Aloha," signed, "Diane." I was so interested in the book that I it read it in only a few hours. It stated that once you experience Aloha, you understand its power to make a better life. Actually, the Aloha Spirit is Hawaiian Law. Here's a quote from the book: "The Aloha Spirit is the coordination of mind and heart within each person. It brings each person to the self. Each person must think and emote good feelings to others."

My tears fell to the pages of the book and I began to understand the Hawaiian way of life. The book's message was my Christmas gift, and her words were the best compliment anyone could have given me.

This recent lesson drew me to volunteer at a Habitat for Humanity house build. The soon-to-be homeowners were a young Hawaiian couple in their mid-twenties, with two small children. They were eager to finish their house and move in, since they had been living in one bedroom of a family member's home for almost three years.

Their new home was adorable – two bedrooms, one bath, and a large living/dining/kitchen combo room. There were four of us working on the inside of the house that day; we primed the interior doors, closet doors, outside deck and steps, and the front porch. Hawaiian homes were different from any homes I had ever seen. The foundations were most often post and pier, which allowed for airflow under the house and kept it cool and dry. Thanks to the consistently nice weather, washers, dryers, and hot water heaters were often outside in a closet, attached to the house, which also kept the home cool and dry. It was fascinating to learn, from an insider's perspective, about Habitat's housing for low-income families. Each potential homeowner must meet a variety of requirements: the family's need for adequate housing, the ability to pay a nominal monthly mortgage, participate in credit counseling, and the willingness to put in 350 sweat equity hours on their home.

I was full of pride and happy to help a family in need, and it reminded me of the first house Chad and I bought. Chad worked full time while earning his master's degree online; I attended a local university full time to earn my undergraduate degree. With one income, money was tight. Our house was sparsely decorated and the living room was empty for several years. Most of the used furnishings we had were given to us by Chad's parents. But it didn't matter to either of us; we had each other. We would often laugh and joke about how broke we were. But we were only broke financially.

I began to shift, and understand what was important in life. It was not the stuff I had accumulated, it was my experiences throughout life… the knowledge I gained, the exposure to something new, the wonderful people who entered my life, and the random acts of kindness I received, and also gave. It was okay not to have every moment of my day planned out. Go with the flow, what feels right at the time. Expect nothing and you won't be disappointed.

One afternoon I enjoyed the cool air-conditioned movie theater. Chad and I rarely went to see a movie on the big screen; we always rented them at home and relaxed on our couch. I think it was partly due to working all week and just wanting to be in our quiet home with each other. After leaving the movie theater, I turned on my cell phone to find a text message from my brother saying that my mom had been in the emergency room for what she thought was her heart. My shaky finger immediately punched in his number. He said that after some tests, including an EKG, the doctor sent her home. Joel said not to say anything to Mom because she didn't want me to worry, since I was so far away and dealing with my own issues. I felt scared and wished I were there with her. So many questions... was she okay, what was happening, would there be additional tests, and how was she dealing with the situation?

I called her at home a little later after I calmed myself down a bit, and neither one of us mentioned her visit to the hospital. I could hear the weakness in her voice, but she said she was just tired. After talking for a few minutes, we told each other we loved each other and hung up. My heart pounded. Was her life in jeopardy? I worried about being so far away, and questioned my ability to deal with anything life-threatening so soon after Chad's death. Over the next few days I kept track of my mom's condition through my brother. I called her every day, but her visit to the ER or any subsequent visits to the doctor were never mentioned.

I rarely remembered my dreams, if I even had them. But the ones I had since Chad's death were violent, strange, and scary. Tommy Lee Jones (yes, the actor) and Steven Tyler from Aerosmith were at a party I attended. On various occasions that evening I caught both of them staring at me, and I looked away when my eyes met theirs. They worked themselves around the room to get closer to where I was standing alone. When they understood that each of them was after the same thing – me – a violent physical fight broke out. I was mortified and ran out of the party, down a long hallway where I entered a small dark room and locked the door behind me. Within minutes, running water gushed in from across the room, it almost swept me off my feet. I caught my balance and began to run, but the more I ran the deeper the water got. I was in fear for my life. I woke suddenly from the thrashing of my legs running in bed. I rolled over and sat up, gasping for air. What was I running from?

The morning air smelled fresh and was cool on my skin, as I stood in the lobby of my condo complex. I looked around and noticed a woman who appeared to be in her forties, carrying a beach bag and walking towards me. Within seconds the shuttle pulled up in front and the two of us boarded. We ended up sitting across from each other and it took no time for us to start talking; I felt an immediate connection. So much so, we barely noticed as the driver stopped at the beach.

We got off the shuttle and decided to spread our towels and sit together on the sand and continue our conversation. We had a lot in common... she was going through a difficult divorce and found her life to be very different and challenging. She and her husband had five kids together; she had given birth to three and two were adopted. She felt like a horrible mom because the kids were stuck in the middle of the adult mess.

Our chatter never slowed as we exchanged stories about nosy friends, people you thought were your friends but abandoned you when things got intense, getting rid of toxic people, making better choices when it came to friends, and people you allow into your inner circle. I found it comforting that someone else who was going through tough times also chose to get away. For me, it was always easier to sort through my emotions and make decisions when I was removed from the situation and outside influences; I had a clearer head. I know people mean well, but sometimes their babble clutters my mind and it makes it more difficult to focus on my thoughts.

Many evenings I sat on the beach and watched the sun slowly lower in the sky. The massive canvas above me turned various shades of orange and the bright yellow spot gradually disappeared, at the same time reappearing as a new day for someone on the other side of the world. In the few seconds it took for the sun to touch the ocean and vanish, I thought about how quickly things can change. I thought about the text from my brother. Was my mom going to be okay? Guilt pulsed through my body... she was there for me and I'm gallivanting thousands of miles away. I wasn't doing anything bad or wrong, but it felt wrong, particularly after everything she had done for me. I was ashamed of my inaction, but I wasn't supposed to even know about her condition. What if she were to die?

Just after the New Year I made reservations for lunch and a tour at the Vanilla Farm. As I drove up the driveway of the farm with my windows down, the vanilla aroma swept through the air and I inhaled deeply, which sparked a sense of ease. I parked the car and walked around the beautiful grounds towards the front porch of a stunning yellow house, which turned out to be the store. Shelves were stocked with vanilla beans, vanilla extract, and an assortment of vanilla-scented body products.

Off the back of the store was a large screened-in porch where lunch would be served. The hostess started calling names to be seated for lunch, and of course everyone was in the company of another person. When she finally called my name, she asked if I objected to sitting with a couple. I told her I didn't mind if they didn't.

Tim and Margo, a husband and wife, were extremely welcoming and I appreciated their kindness. Margo had attended a work conference and they chose to extend their stay to explore the island. She was an oncologist and Tim was a sleep specialist. Of all the people to sit with, an oncologist. I felt anxiety build as I reflected on the other oncologists I knew... Dr. C, Dr. B, and Dr. H, all of Chad's doctors. I fought back the tears as I asked Margo her specialty, and she replied, "radiology." She seemed happy as she talked about her life in Nashville with family and friends. Lunch arrived and the dialogue shifted to the delicious food.

I said good-bye to my lunch friends and started my drive back to Kona. I began to realize I wanted to be strong. And I wanted people to believe I was strong. And maybe I appeared strong on the outside. But when a similar or tough situation presented itself, I crumbled on the inside. This was a behavior ingrained into me during the ten most physically demanding weeks of my life at Fort Jackson, South Carolina – a United States Army Installation that operated Basic Combat Training for new soldiers. And for the following eight years of my military service it was a basic survival skill… do not appear to be weak, or lack strength, or display an inability to manage during any situation. That could get you killed.

One afternoon I couldn't resist: an open house. The car just took me in that direction, and stopped curbside. As I walked through the front door the realtor greeted me. He was in his mid-fifties, with a pleasant demeanor and a welcoming smile. He immediately started rattling off details of the condo – association fees, layout, electric bill, taxes, location, and amenities of the complex. It was a gorgeously updated one-bedroom, two-bath, oceanfront condo. He handed me the condo specifications as I walked out the door. I looked, out of curiosity. What would it cost, monthly, to buy and maintain a home here? What a dream, to own an oceanfront condo in Hawaii. Yeah, right!

One of my last evenings in Hawaii, I came across a small oceanfront bar. I went in and grabbed a table. The longer I sat the more captivated I became with the gentleman who was singing. He was in his mid-to-late thirties, slender, with short brown hair. He wore shorts, a short-sleeved button up Hawaiian shirt, and flip flops (in Hawaii they are called slippers) – the usual Hawaiian attire. His voice was strong, soulful, and raspy; he reminded me of Joe Cocker, and he could *really* play the guitar.

His music brought me happiness… my body swayed and my right foot tapped to the beat. Eventually I found myself almost dancing in my seat. His lyrics were about struggles, happy times, rough times, sadness, lovers, challenges, and the gamut of emotions that go along with all of it.

I bought two CD's from Pete Kartsounes that evening and listened to nothing else for the next several days. There was one song I listened to repeatedly, until I memorized every word. Then I studied each verse until I understood what it was saying to me. Here's an excerpt: "Set out driving down a country road, don't care how long or where it'll go, bound to somehow kiss my soul and free my mind. Chorus: "If time is the sand, dreams are the ocean and angels stand by our sides, do what you can to sing your own song and live out your dreams, while the band plays on."

These powerful words put my life together. As much as I had been thinking about my dreams, moving on, and where to go, it was not until I listened to this song that I really understood what moving on meant. Here's how I interpreted those lyrics:

"Driving down a country road" – Driving down the road of life.

"Don't care how long" – I have no control how long I'll be on this earth.

"Or where it goes" – I had no control of Chad's death, but I can control where some of my own life goes.

"Bound to somehow kiss my soul" – Love myself for who I am.

"And free my mind" – Release the negativity and have positive thoughts.

"Time is the sand" – Each second of the day is like one granule of sand; eventually they will run out.

"Dreams are the ocean" – My dreams are as big as I make them, like the grandness of the ocean.

"And angels stand by our sides" – Chad is with me.

"Do what you can to sing your own song" – Live my life the way I want.

"And live out your dreams" – Make my dreams happen.

"While the band plays on" – Life continues to play whether you are in it or not; don't get stuck in your situation because life will pass you by.

These last few weeks in Hawaii, as I observed my fiftieth birthday, Christmas, and the New Year, I began to enjoy myself. Was this okay? Could I smile and grieve at the same time? Or does one eventually surpass the other? I would have preferred Chad be in paradise with me, but since he couldn't, I fulfilled our dream alone. On occasion, I had brief thoughts of him flying in separately, meeting me at the condo or the airport. But maybe he did come to Hawaii with me, in the only way he could, by sending life experiences my way to put the pieces together.

Chapter 13

EMOTIONAL THROWBACK

As I walked into my cold house in Syracuse, my stomach clenched into knots. This was my reality – no one to welcome me with open arms. The last time someone hugged me was several weeks earlier, when the concierge in Hawaii wrapped her arms around me after I blurted out I was a widow.

Memories and emotions flooded in as I walked around the house... the dining room furniture Chad loved, the granite counter tops he had carefully selected, the coat rack he made, his animal print blanket tossed over the arm of the couch. I was thrown back into the emptiness and a paralyzed physical state. I was confused as chaos churned inside me. Just fifteen hours ago I stood smiling on a warm, sunny, sandy beach, not wanting to return to Syracuse. Feeling numb, I drove south on Interstate 81 and got off at the Adams/Harrison Street exit, headed towards the medical heart of Syracuse. I had made this drive many times before and was on automatic pilot, giving no thought to anything. It was that time of year, my routine annual exams, and I was just going through the motions to get there.

As I turned onto Irving Avenue, a frightening sensation radiated through my body. There, to my right, was the hospital where Chad passed away. It was difficult to look at. Even knowing I was on the same street as this massive building made me feel sick. My emotional state took another dive, back to when Chad was hospitalized there. I pictured myself in the chapel praying to God; I pictured Chad's cool lifeless body in the hospital bed, and the nurse pronouncing his death.

A flash of multiple emotions from that day penetrated my thoughts – guilt, sadness, heartache, and shock. It felt as if my heart stopped, and I coughed to somehow stun it back into regular rhythm. Through the uncontrollable heavy breathing and tears I managed to park the car in the parking garage across the street from the hospital. Good... the site that brought such deep pain had disappeared behind the concrete walls. I sat in the driver's seat and sobbed, pulling tissue after tissue from my purse. Eventually, as the tears slowed and the sharp pain began to ease, I pulled down the sun visor and opened the mirror. The skin around my eyes was bright red, the whites of my eyes were glassy and filled with tiny red blood vessels, and dark mascara was smudged under both eyes. My hand shook as I wiped away the mascara. I took a deep breath and convinced myself I would be okay.

As I walked in the medical building, adjacent to the hospital, I hung my head as I maneuvered the maze of hallways to my doctor's office. Once I entered the waiting room I signed my name on the sheet at reception and buried my face in my cell phone, where no one could see me. When the visit was over, I couldn't get out of there fast enough.

Susan and I were meeting at Daniella's Steakhouse for dinner and drinks at the bar. I was tense as I drove the five miles to the restaurant, but I tried not to overthink the situation. Relax Leah... take a deep breath. As I pulled into the parking lot, a numbing sensation slowly consumed every inch of my body. I closed my eyes and tried to control my emotions with slow steady breathing. Daniella's was a major part of my Friday evenings with Chad; it was our preferred end-of-the-week dinner spot. I sat in the car for several minutes before I gained the courage to even open the car door. Come on Leah... one step at a time. Anxiety exploded from my chest as I walked towards the restaurant. For a split second, I thought I would turn around and go home, but no, this was something I needed to do. With a lump in my throat, I swung open the door, took a deep breath, and walked in.

The dinner lights were low and a faint familiar sound of smooth jazz music played in the background. I frantically scanned the small, elegant dining room. What was I afraid of? Running into an acquaintance? Or was it excitement, thinking I would find somehow Chad there?

There were a few empty tables, one of which was a two-top in the right corner; it was where Chad and I normally enjoyed dinner. I imagined us sitting there again, sharing the homemade carrot cake we loved and discussing our plans for the next day. I stared and stood motionless. Charlie, the owner, swiftly walked over and greeted me with a kiss on the cheek and a long warm hug. "Great to see you," he said. I half grinned and slightly nodded.

"Great to see you too," I replied.

He took my arm and walked me to the bar where he pulled out a chair, and I sat down. Brian, the bartender, walked around the bar with a huge smile and gave me a hug and kiss. "You want your usual?" he asked.

"Sure," I said, as if this was a regular day at my favorite restaurant.

Then I felt a soft tap on my right shoulder, and Susan pulled out the bar stool next to me... we smiled and embraced. "I missed you," Susan whispered in my ear.

"You too."

Susan ordered a glass of wine, and we clinked glasses and cheered to health, happiness, and great friends. She was eager to hear about Hawaii, which was our conversation through the first glass of wine. At some point, Susan gently touched my right forearm as it lay on the bar and looked me in the eye. "Are you okay? We can leave if you want."

"I'm comfortable and calm; I'm okay," I replied.

The anticipated arrival at Daniella's was much worse than actually being there. Susan and I ordered dinner and finished out the evening talking about family, friends, and life. We hugged and exchanged "I love you's" and went our separate ways. As I drove home that evening, my thoughts wandered to Chad. I missed him, he had so much more to accomplish, and I was not ready to let him go. My vision became impaired by the tears of profound sadness; I sobbed all the way home.

I was eternally grateful for the time I had with Chad. He loved me, I know that. He would often say, "Do you realize I love you more than anything?" I miss that. I miss lying next to him at night and feeling his heart beat on my hand that lay across his bare chest. He was my rock; he was courageous, confident, controlled, and always had a purpose that he was committed to. I needed to believe I could empower myself to move on. But would a move forward be possible in Syracuse? Something in Hawaii gave me the ability to begin the transformation of myself and my life. But now, back in Syracuse, my emotions were like a runaway train. I thought I would never be able to rein them in, as the emotional chaos was overwhelming.

Lynne, my BFF, and her husband, Bob, were always inviting me to dinner at their house. Lynne and I would make a salad, set the table, have a glass of wine, and laugh about something silly, while Bob grilled outside on the back deck. The three of us enjoyed our meal, while having meaningful conversations, and after dessert we would most often play a dice game. Bob always seemed to win, but Lynne and I never gave up. We danced around our chairs and would send positive energy to each other while talking to the dice, in hopes of beating Bob. Throughout the evening I closely watched the interactions between the two of them. "I'll make the salad, I'll grill, what can I get you to drink, I talked to your mom, what happened at work today?" I realized even more how much Chad's absence was impacting my daily life. These moments made me feel more alone and hollow. Broken. Each time I left their house, the weeping started as I backed out of their driveway, and it didn't stop until I arrived home and crawled into bed with my knees up to my chin and the covers over my head.

In almost twenty years of living there I had made many friends in Syracuse. Chad would laugh and shake his head whenever we were out somewhere because I always knew someone. He would ask, "How do you know all these people?"

"It's who I am," I said.

I enjoyed making new friends and rarely met a stranger. But now I had zero connection to Syracuse, other than my friends. Happily their lives continued as usual, although I had no idea what that was for me anymore.

Living in the house was growing more uncomfortable every day. Things were maybe too familiar… the curtains Chad hung, the artwork we picked out, and the floor plan of the house we selected and built. Every corner reminded me of him, even the paint color on the walls. Perhaps sections of the house were too painful and that's why I isolated myself to three rooms – the kitchen, master bedroom (where I was unconsciously aware of my surroundings while I slept), and the bathroom. I started to realize that our beautiful home was no longer my beautiful dream house. I began to think more and more about moving. Should I move? Could I move? Where would I move?

The next several weeks I explored the demographics of various cities, and my likes and dislikes. I designed a spreadsheet that outlined my monthly budget and what I could afford, and obsessively searched the intenet for properties. My intuition had been fairly accurate over the years and this decision seemed to come surprisingly easily. It felt right. No worries or conflicts surfaced. When I make a decision, I don't get caught up in the minutia of how to get to the end result because it clutters my mind and then I'm not able to make the decision at all. I make the best-educated decision I can at the time and trust that the details will work out later. What's the worst thing that could happen? If I'm not happy with my decision I'll make another decision to change it. Decisions are not mistakes, they're learning experiences. Every day I'm presented with choices, and it's those decisions to step through the door or not that determine my life.

There are not many decisions I regret, and I am grateful to be able to say that I have a tremendous number of life experiences. This was a giant step for me... my decision to move out of New York State.

Chapter 14

ONGOING GRIEF WITH HAPPIER TIMES

Two months earlier I had promised Michelle, a friend from high school, that I would not miss the April renewal of her wedding vows to her husband Steve, in Idaho. But first, I wanted to visit my twenty-three-year-old nephew, Witt, in Las Vegas. He was recovering from brain surgery and treatment.

After I grabbed my luggage in baggage claim at McCarran International Airport, I called the phone number Witt had given me. The gentleman said he would meet me just outside baggage claim and give me a ride to my destination. As I stood near the curb and waited, I noticed a dark stretch limo pull into the pick-up area, and saw a tall, middle-aged man step out, announcing he was picking up Leah Goodman. I looked around to see if there was another Leah Goodman... this wasn't for me, it couldn't be.

The limo driver said my name again and I strolled over to investigate the situation. It was true, Witt had sent a limo just for me. The driver loaded my luggage into the cavernous trunk and I climbed into the back seat of this mammoth twelve-passenger limo, fully equipped with leather, lights, and mirrors. As the driver pulled away, I called my nephew and expressed my gratitude for such a luxurious ride. He replied, "You deserve it." I did deserve happiness and excitement, and I needed to remember that.

Witt and I dined out that evening at a steakhouse on the Vegas strip. As the young waitress took our drink order, she looked at Witt and asked, "Did you lose a bet?"

He looked at her a bit confused, and she said, "You're bald."

Witt firmly replied, "No, I had a brain tumor."

I guess she didn't notice the six-inch scar running down the back of his head. The waitress's eyes enlarged, her eyebrows pushed up into her forehead, and she apologized profusely. I was embarrassed for her, and felt hurt for Witt.

Only five months earlier he was rolled into the operating room at Duke University in North Carolina, had his skull opened, and a germinoma tumor removed. Then, shortly after surgery, he endured five weeks of whole-brain radiation. Now, Witt was the same happy, funny, and loving nephew he was before surgery. I felt blessed to be a part of his life. He was a great inspiration by staying positive and strong, and it encouraged me to do the same. As Las Vegas faded away in my rear-view mirror, I thought about the second chance Witt was given. Not everyone is that fortunate.

Most of the drive northeast was flat, treeless, and lifeless. I found entertainment in the car radio; it blared loudly as I sang karaoke at the top of my lungs and pounded out the beat of the music on the steering wheel. I drove for approximately six hours and was just outside Salt Lake City, Utah, when I pulled into the parking lot of a small local restaurant. I arrived on time.

As I walked through the front door, I noticed Amy sitting in the back of the small dining room. We made eye contact and walked towards each other with huge smiles. Only a few months earlier we had bonded in Hawaii, in part because we were both going through a tough time. For the next two hours we talked about our lives. Her kids were doing much better since the divorce, I had decided to move out of New York, she bought a small quaint house, I had cut some toxic people out of my life, and so did she. In just a few months, both of us had clearly taken steps to move forward. Our brief visit ended too soon, but I still had another five-hour drive.

As I continued across Utah, into Idaho, I again realized the empowerment I gained by being out of the familiarity of Syracuse and my home there. The accumulation of experiences over the last few months led me to a positive, independent, and secure feeling about myself and my future, which made me more comfortable in making life-changing decisions.

The last time I saw Steve and Michelle was our thirtieth high school reunion, almost two years earlier. It was late when I arrived at their home, but both waited up. It was an emotional greeting for Michelle and me; her mother passed away of lung cancer only six weeks after I lost Chad. We hugged, we cried, and we stared at each other. It was a mutual understanding; the grief was something we shared.

The next morning, I heard muffled voices through my closed bedroom door. I heard Michelle's voice, Steve's laugh, and Michelle's father Ed's familiar voice. Michelle and I spent a lot of time at each other's homes growing up, and got to know the other's parents, and Ed was like my second father. Steve and Michelle married not long after high school and moved to Idaho, where they raised their two boys. By now, I smelled coffee and heard strong belly laughs coming from the kitchen. From the hallway, I peeked around the corner and saw the three of them standing around the island in the kitchen. As I approached, they all turned towards me and said, "Good morning!" Ed and I held each other tightly. It had been over thirty years since we had seen each other. Our embrace was much more than a greeting, it was a comforting form of affection. Ed had lost his wife eight months earlier, a pain I was familiar with.

Chad always gave me a hard time about weddings because I cried at every one I attended. They reminded me of my own wedding, the love that was expressed on that day and the lifetime commitment made to one another... to have and to hold, from this day forward, for better, for worse, for richer, for poorer, in sickness and in health, to love and cherish, until death do us part. This deeply touches my heart.

Several years earlier Chad and I were on vacation in the Bahamas and I stood in the oceanfront window of our room and observed a wedding that took place on the beach. I couldn't hear one word, but I watched and cried as they stared at each other, slipped rings on each other's fingers, and kissed. "You are now husband and wife."

My body tingled with excitement at the display of love. I didn't know them, but I still wished them the love and happiness I experienced on a daily basis.

Chad gently pulled me away from the window and said, "That's enough."

He didn't like to see me cry.

Michelle and I, and her younger sister Linda, had makeup strewn all over Michelle's bed, and we each had our own mirror, brushing on eye shadow and mascara. We laughed about our spring break adventures in Florida, many years ago, and that we got so sunburned it made us sick. Linda checked her watch and reminded us that we had only thirty minutes to be dressed and ready for the ceremony.

Michelle reminisced about this day, thirty-one years ago. She didn't have a wedding dress and she wanted one this time, a simple one. Her voice shook slightly as she talked about her two boys standing up with Steve. Linda and I reached out and gave her a hug.

Tears trickled down Michelle's face as she said, "I wish Cindy were here to celebrate with us."

Cindy was Michelle's older sister who had passed away about twenty years earlier. She thanked me for making the trip and being part of her special day. I smiled. I was honored.

Steve gently knocked on the door and said, "It's time to get going."

As the wedding party arrived at the church, we entered through the side door and patiently waited in a small room down the hall from the nave. There were a lot of whispers and small talk, and abruptly Michelle said, "I wish we renewed our vows last year. Mom would have been here with us." My heart sank into my stomach; I was so sad for her at that moment. Just then, the minister cracked the door and softly said, "It's time."

One by one, we quietly filed out of the room and took our place in the hallway. Michael (Michelle and Steve's youngest son) and I were first to walk down the aisle. All of a sudden, my palms were sweaty and my heart pounded hard. As the music started Michael looked at me, put his left arm out, and I hooked my right arm into his. Then he said, "I'm so glad you wore low heels, I'm taller than you." That swept away all my nervous feelings and I began to laugh. We stepped into the nave as I attempted to contain my amusement. The guests saw a huge smile on my face as Michael escorted me down the aisle.

As we approached the front of the church, he gently took my arm from his... I was in place. Michael looked me in the eye, nodded his head, and turned to take his place across from me. My jaws tensed as Linda and Scotty, Steve and Michelle's oldest son, approached, and Linda took her place next to me. I stared over the crowd as Michelle and Ed appeared in the doorway. My head began to throb as I attempted to hold back the tears. It was that wedding feeling... love, commitment, and a lifetime together. I broke out in a sweat; single droplets ran along my spine and I bent my knees slightly in hopes I wouldn't pass out.

I briefly flashed to my father handing me off to Chad. They were now both deceased. Ed and Michelle stopped short of the chancel where Steve stepped down to take the hand of his bride. Ed graciously let Michelle go and sat down in the pew to my right. He looked up at me and grinned, then reached out and handed me two tissues. I wiped my eyes and wrapped the damp tissues around my bouquet.

My mind flipped back to my wedding day... we stood face to face before the minister. I was nervous and so was Chad. I could see it in his eyes and hear it in his voice as we exchanged vows. Tears lightly flowed down my face, and we gently slipped rings on each other's ring finger. Then the minister introduced us. Mr. and Mrs. Goodman.

As I watched Steve and Michelle leave the church, arm in arm, I was grateful to be a part of this loving event and extraordinary family. It brought back happy memories of our long-term friendship, reminding me that those joyful times would have to be more frequent. They might be the source of my survival.

Over the next few days, Steve, Michelle, and I saw the sights of downtown Boise, the blue football field at Boise State, and the botanical gardens that were beginning to bloom. We crashed into each other at the go-cart track and laughed at almost everything. We honestly enjoyed being together, even sitting in their living room watching TV.

It was an incredible trip out west, and I was beginning to awaken from the grief I was so deeply buried in since my return from Hawaii. It was daily torture to struggle with grief and wanting to fulfill my happiness, but I was continuing to crack open my heart to a whole new world.

Chapter 15

YOU'RE DOING WHAT?

As I hung up the phone, my palms dripped with sweat. The realtor's last words were, "I'll get the paperwork ready."

I had just asked him to make an offer on a waterfront condo in Kailua-Kona, Hawaii. I had briefly seen this condo several months earlier, and it needed a lot of work. But if I could get it at the price I wanted, I would have money for renovations. Good fortune was on my side; no other potential buyer had made an inquiry.

Even though Chad and I had bought several homes over the years, I was nervous about "my" first time. Was I doing the right thing? Would my offer be accepted, and what if it wasn't? Chad and I would have discussed this purchase in detail before making an offer. That would have helped put my mind at ease, but since I didn't have that option, I went with my instincts... to go for it!

Negotiation is the process by which everyone will compromise to some degree to hopefully reach an agreement. No matter my desires, the seller would not agree unless I solved her problem or eased her situation. However, I had a budget and would defend my ground. Two days after my initial offer my cell phone rang. It was a number that began with 808, the Hawaii area code. I jumped up from my chair and stared at the screen for several seconds before answering. My realtor called to tell me the owner counter-offered and didn't budge from her original price. I was disappointed; in my opinion she was asking way too much for a condo that needed thousands of dollars in renovations. Plus, her price didn't work into my budget.

I took twenty-four hours to think about her offer before I countered back, with not much more than my original offer, claiming this was the highest I would go. Take it or leave it. Surprisingly, I stayed emotionally neutral – no excitement, no fear, I remained calm. I had to be willing to walk away if she didn't agree to my maximum price. It was a bold move on my part, but I didn't want to play the back-and-forth game.

Two days later, I received confirmation that the seller agreed to my purchase price. I was the owner of a one-bedroom, one-bathroom, oceanfront condo in Hawaii. My emotions were mixed – excited to be moving, but sad that I would be going without my husband. This was the beginning of my commitment to myself. It meant facing my fears, dealing with challenges, embracing change, acceptance, being comfortable with my emotions, and confronting life head on. But now, how was I going to tell both sides of my family and my friends, and would they understand? I had to make them understand.

What I began to understand was that I felt "touched" by Hawaii. My psyche was free, unleashed from the confines of my grief. It was a sort of spiritual connection, like I was called to move there, as if I were guided there. Was it a love for an island that gave me new meaning in life?

In part, it was the Aloha spirit, to express my love, caring, kindness, and gratitude to myself and others. I flourished in Hawaii and felt suppressed in Syracuse. Hawaii was sacred and I was honored; something I did not feel on the mainland. Everyone respected each other, even small children, teenagers, and middle-aged strangers. The land was valued and loved. It felt alive. The royalty of ancient times came to life in songs, dance, and stories. The rhythm of the Hawaiian music danced in my heart. The saltwater breeze kissed my face. The sand connected me to a powerful healing energy. And the sound of the ocean bonded with my soul. The island gave me passion for life once again.

My daily conversations with my mom and mother-in-law included a detailed description of how I missed the island... the most beautiful place in the world, perfect weather, laid back lifestyle, cultural experience, so much to do outside, so much to learn, and the beautiful blue-green ocean. They were the ones I worried about the most. But I realized that it didn't matter; I knew what was good for me, and I was going to do it. The buildup of admiration for the island was preparation for eventually breaking the news of my upcoming move. As many times as I tried to explain the Hawaiian way, I'm not sure they truly understood.

Chad's death turned my world upside down. Death was something that happened to old people, not when you're forty-five. His death knocked me out of my comfort zone, and a harsh lesson was learned. We only get one life. Live with no regrets and don't put off your dreams, because they may never happen. Aloha was in my heart, it brought me peace, contentment, and happiness. I had to leave behind the familiar and move forward into the unknown, and that meant becoming fully engaged in the present. I had to take charge of my future and erase the old definition of myself and begin to define my new self. Since the "Practice Aloha" book gave me much insight into the Aloha spirit, I hoped it would do the same for my family and friends. So, I ordered twelve copies and began to distribute them as gifts.

I thought my mom would understand; she and my military father moved many times throughout their marriage and lived thousands of miles away from family on more than one occasion. She may not like the idea of me living so far away, but she had always been supportive and allowed me to live my life. My brother would be a different story... he only made two moves as a military brat: the first one was before he started kindergarten, and the second was going into eighth grade. Joel never made another move, and he and his family have never lived more than a few miles from most of their relatives and where they grew up. Living thousands of miles away was incomprehensible to them.

I was more concerned about the Goodman side because I never wanted them to think I was abandoning them. But I was also worried it might be too painful for me to live close to them. It could be a constant reminder to his family that Chad is no longer on this earth, and I am. Would I be resented? They had been part of my family for the past twenty years and I wanted our relationship to continue. Each of them had a familiar piece of Chad... stories told by the nieces and nephews of how Chad taught them to fish or showed them a high-tech karate move; siblings recounting a childhood memory of how they got caught throwing horse manure at a convertible car; and my mother-in-law describing how much Chad was just like his father. Chad would always be a part of my life and I felt the same about his family.

The decision to move so far away had many factors but the most important one was that it was something for me. I loved the Hawaiian weather and way of life, and felt it would be the best place for me to work through my grief without any outside influences. As far back as I can remember I didn't like people telling me what to do, how to do it, and when to do it; I liked it even less now. I needed to awaken to my higher purpose, and Hawaii was that place, my place to heal and move on.

Cindi, my therapist, was very supportive of my decision to move, but she had one question. "What was it about Hawaii?" So, I gave her a copy of the Practice Aloha book and explained that Hawaiians live to do the right thing for themselves, others, and the environment; the Aloha way created an atmosphere of friendliness and love; Hawaiians lived outdoors – open air restaurants, open shopping areas, and beaches, large windows and lanais; Hawaiians believed in life energy, which meant enjoying those around them and carrying out meaningful acts; they also did not focus on material possessions. Hawaii was a community. At the end of my session, she said, "Leah, your eyes lit up when you talked about Hawaii and I heard the passion in your voice."

Chad and Leah at a 1960's fundraiser with her '69 Chevelle.

Chad and Leah

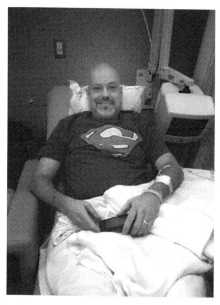

Chad receiving his first chemo treatment.

Chad fishing the Kapushka River on the Kamchatka
Peninsula in Russia.

Chapter 16

ONE-YEAR MARK

For the last fourteen years, around mid-to-late July, I would become aware of an "upset" feeling, but didn't fully understand why. Then one day it hit me and it all fell into place... my dad had passed away on August 10, 1997.

I had subconsciously been mourning my loss. Did my mind and body remember the pain and it's somehow marked in the cells of my body, and the grief resurfaces at some point? Was that trigger his last hospital admission, my flight from Syracuse to Kentucky, or the ambulance ride from my parents' home to the hospital, where I tearfully watched my dad's face through the rear-door window of the ambulance as I followed behind in my mom's car? Would I have the same pattern of feelings with Chad?

The one-year mark (I refused to call it an anniversary because that was something you celebrated) was near and I found myself cringing every time I looked at the calendar to see how many more days until that day.

I tried to recall the details of those days prior to Chad's death. Did we watch DVD's about our National Parks? Did the Reiki Master help him relax? Maybe it was the day his room was filled with family and friends and we told stories and laughed, or maybe he didn't feel very well, so he slept all day. I was thrown back into an extreme emotional state for two weeks prior to that dreaded day, but it was a place I needed to be. I wanted to feel the deep pain that helped me remember, because I never wanted to forget. Accepting Chad's death was difficult and at times felt like a roller coaster ride with extreme fluctuations in highs and lows and ups and downs. But, over time, the difficult periods had become less intense and were shorter in duration.

Cindi explained to me that special occasions and holidays may bring about a strong sense of grief and she said to give myself time to adjust and recover, be respectful of my grief. For days, I felt sad and frightened about my future, and at times I felt lonely. When I cried, I was mostly alone; I felt the need to protect my family and friends by putting on a brave face. I didn't want them to worry about me.

I reminded myself of both the good times and the not-so-good times by going through many items I had tucked away. One was a large, decorative grayish blue gift box I pulled from underneath the end table in the living room. It contained hundreds of cards that Chad had received during his illness. As I held the box, it gave me a strange feeling... I wasn't sure if I wanted to open it.

I sat down on the couch and placed the box next to me, then slowly opened the lid and peeked in. The cards were piled on top of each other and scattered about in a disorganized manner. I pushed the lid all the way open and stared at the cards on top. Eventually, I grabbed a few cards and put them on my lap. They were a reminder of the tough times, but also represented the concern and love people had for Chad.

I picked up one card and read it; it was from one of Chad's co-workers. She sent him a card every week with a friendly note, and lottery tickets generously tucked inside. It was a reminder that I was not the only one to lose Chad. I cried as I picked up another card – it was from several of Chad's co-workers. Each one had written a short note of inspiration and signed his or her name. The next several cards were from various co-workers, friends, and family members; they extended wishes of hope for a speedy recovery. I took a deep breath as I reached into the big box again and pulled out a three-inch-ring blue binder that I remembered well.

Many of Chad's co-workers had placed items into the binder, in separate clear plastic sheet protectors. There were pictures of people from different departments, a poem someone wrote, a beautiful winter scene someone drew. One page was filled with cutouts of Chad's favorite things... Cheerios, SpaghettiOs, and Halva. Another page was muddy paw prints from one of the therapy dogs; another was filled with superheroes with a picture of Chad's head placed on the shoulders on each superhero's body. Some pages were private jokes that I didn't understand, and others were shared memories.

As I read every word that was written and I ran my hand across each page, I felt their love, their hope, and many prayers. Before I turned the page, I wiped away the tears that dropped onto the plastic sheets. I closed the blue binder and put the cards back in the box. That was enough for now.

I walked down the hallway to my bedroom where I was drawn to a particular dresser drawer. I sat on the floor Indian style in front of Chad's dresser, closed my eyes, and inhaled deeply a few times. Should I open this drawer? I stared at the bottom drawer for several seconds, then reached out with both hands and placed one on each knob, slowly opening the drawer. On top was a red knit hat Chad had worn during his radiation treatments. I picked it up gently and pressed it into my face, hoping to get a slight scent of Chad. I placed the hat in my lap and hung my head, brushing off the tears that fell. I glanced again at the drawer and noticed a pair of Christmas socks decorated with the Grinch, one of Chad's favorite characters. I unrolled them and remembered a young nephew begging Chad for his Christmas socks one year. I gently rolled them back up.

I reached for a tissue on the nearby nightstand and wiped the tears from my eyes. Chad would never wear these clothes again... I cried harder, my head throbbed, and my chest felt like an erupting volcano, spewing emotions everywhere. One of my favorites was an orange polo shirt; Chad wore it when we had our picture taken together on Myrtle Beach in South Carolina. I held the shirt up by the shoulders and imagined that Chad would fill that shirt again. How did I live every single day for twenty years with the love of my life and then one day... poof? Gone... forever? How does one's mind deal with that? How do I get through it? Just when I thought my tears ducts were empty and my head would burst from the pounding headache, I saw a blue t-shirt.

A cool tingling sensation ran up my spine. It was the shirt Chad wore to his first chemotherapy treatment, with a large Superman emblem on the front. The memory of that day is etched in my mind forever: Chad reclining in a chair with an IV needle stuck in his left arm, while the drugs slowly dripped into his body. I pulled my legs into my chest and wrapped both arms around my bent knees, clenching all the clothes I had pulled from the drawer. I placed my forehead on top of my knees and tried to breathe through the stuttered sobs. Was it a few seconds, minutes, or an hour? I don't recall. As I stood up, the beautiful wooden box of Chad's ashes stood before me on the top of the dresser. I carefully opened it and looked at the small picture of Chad in the lid. With bloodshot, swollen eyes I gave him a slight smile back. I imagined him saying, "You've been crying." I told him I loved him and missed him every day. I wiped the tears from my face and smiled at him. I softly closed the lid and walked away as I clutched the heart pendant that lay on my chest.

That dreaded day was here and I decided to stay home, away from people, away from friends, away from family… I wanted to be alone. I wanted the freedom to break down in private, or stay in bed all day, or kick and scream, or cry. I wanted to do what I was feeling that day, no more, no less. I was awake but still lying in bed that morning when I heard the garage door open. It could only be David, Chad's best friend. He stopped by on his way to work to check on me, not only to give me support, but to receive it. We hugged each other tightly without saying a word; we knew what drew us together that day – the love we shared for Chad, the deep pain we felt, the empathy we had for each other, the respect we gave each other, and the many years of memories we shared. David and I stood in the kitchen as we talked about Chad for over an hour, mostly about how much we missed him. David's voice was brittle as he described how he had not been fishing or hunting in the last year because his best friend, the only one he did these activities with, was no longer around. He said, "It's just too painful." I explained that I was in the same situation with the house… it was just too painful to stay here. David finally said that he needed to get to work, he just wanted to make sure I was okay. David always checked on me, not just today. I think he felt an obligation to some degree, watching out for his best friend's widow. But we, too, were best friends; he was like having another brother.

I crawled back into bed, curled up in the fetal position, and cried. I finally realized that this continued behavior would keep me in a depressed state and result in a throbbing headache, not a place I wanted to be. So, I turned on the TV and found a movie – *Mrs. Doubtfire*. Chad loved that movie. I laughed as I watched and remembered the three or four times we watched it together. But my mind wandered off, to those six horrific months of diagnosis, treatment, dying, and finally death. I tried to relive one single day slowly in my mind, minute-by-minute, hour-by-hour. Chad did not eat breakfast that morning, my mom and Chad's mom arrived at the hospital, I barely ate any lunch, the walk to the chapel, calling close friends to say, "You might want to visit soon because he won't last long," and at 3:29 pm when he took his last breath. Those visions are forever ingrained into my memory… his frail motionless body lying in the hospital bed, an IV stuck in his powerless arm, his protruding chest struggling for every breath, and the clear oxygen tubes that stretched across his face and inserted into his nostrils. I recalled how scary and unsettling this time was. But I had to keep in mind that he no longer had to fight to breathe or struggle with pain and nausea or wrestle with his mind about the fact he was dying. The "one year mark" was a torturous struggle, but with the many phone calls from friends and family I made it through.

My perspective on life was once again shifting. I needed to be honest with myself, and discover my true feelings. This was my time to heal and accept the changes that were happening in my life. I had to venture forward into this strange and new world. If I stayed in my grief, unwilling to make the leap, I would not reap the benefits of this difficult passage. What did I have to lose? There was much to gain.

Chapter 17

WHERE TO START?

Not only did I need to sort through Chad's belongings, but every item in the house. With my impending move to Hawaii there were thousands of things I needed to touch, decide where they would go, and then get them there. I read on the internet that it was wise to take one room at a time, and since the living space was sacred, I decided to begin in the basement.

The unfinished basement was where Chad spent much of his leisure time, particularly during the cold winter months. Most of the items in the basement were Chad's – things he bought, used, held... his stuff.

I stood in front of Chad's workshop and stared. I could feel his strong presence. I was surrounded by hundreds of different objects and had no clue what many of them were, or what they were used for. They ranged from really big things, like the freestanding band saw, table saw, and scroll saw, to items you could place in your pocket. On his workbench were two battery-operated drills with the batteries plugged in, two vices – one attached to each side of the bench, and several coffee cans filled with miscellaneous screws, bolts, and nails. Underneath the bench were three large plastic cases. One housed a circular saw, one a sawzall, and the other tool... no clue what it was. As I looked to the right, there were two floor-to-ceiling wood cabinets. I reached up and opened one door, and then the other. All the shelves were unorganized and jammed with cans and jars of nails and screws, containers filled with zip ties, several extension cords, many pairs of heavy work gloves, cleaning rags, paint cans, paint pans and rollers, three hand sanders, a dozen packages of sandpaper, and another one hundred items I couldn't identify.

I took a deep breath and walked away. I was overwhelmed. From one of the many boxes I had distributed throughout the house, I plucked several tissues, one right after the other, and wiped away the tears. I sat down at the dining room table, in Chad's chair, and stared across the living room. Then one of my favorites memories surfaced.

Chad had carefully designed, cut out, and fit together a seated wooden bi-plane with wheels for one of our young nephews. He spent hours in the basement making the gift a perfect piece of art. Together we sanded the individual pieces and then I painted the plane red, blue, and black. Chad was proud of that plane, his masterpiece, and I was proud of him for making it. My body stung with sadness as I clasped my hands together and hung my head. There would be no more memories created in his workshop.

Days later I made another attempt in the basement, this time taking a box of tissue with me. My numb body stood in front of the large gun safe and I just stared. I wasn't even sure how to open it or what exactly was in it. I broke out in a nervous sweat as I inhaled deeply... what was I going to do with this? I wiped my damp palms on the thighs of my jeans and pulled my cell phone from my back pocket, dialing David's number. He picked up on the second ring.

He said, "Oh yes, the combination is the year you two were married."

Words could not flow from my mouth; they were balled together and stuck in my throat. I disconnected the call without another word. My knees buckled as I crumbled to the cement floor. I stayed there and negotiated. "Pull it together, Leah. You will never be able to move forward if you constantly take steps back into the past." The pain was still so tender.

I finally put my energy into standing, and then continued to walk around the basement. A large four-shelf unit that stood on the other side of the basement contained tackle boxes, reels, countless boxes of fishing line, and lots of plastic compartment containers filled with hooks, sinkers, weights, and bobbers.

Next to the shelf unit stood the large wooden handmade rod holder I bought when we lived in Washington State and had given Chad for his birthday many years ago; it was overflowing with various sizes and types of rods. Several five-gallon white buckets were filled with ice fishing gear: tip ups, poles, reels; and leaning against the wall was a hand ice auger. Hanging from the rafters was a personal floatation pontoon boat Chad had used only once.

During the spring and fall months, it was common to find a note on the kitchen counter when I arrived home after work: "I went to the river to fish, be back later." Chad also tied his own flies and always had a large variety on hand for his fishing excursions. Chad took such pleasure in making the plans, buying the airline tickets, practicing with his fly rod and a hula-hoop in the back yard, but most of all he loved the camaraderie. I had to focus on the fact that Chad enjoyed many trips with his family and friends over his lifetime.

One long wall was jam-packed with three large floor-to-ceiling wooden bookshelves, stuffed with various types of books. Chad saved almost every book he had ever touched – schoolbooks, college books, military manuals, woodworking, fishing, hunting, science fiction, true crime, military history, non-fiction, and home repairs. There were large books, small books, hardcover books, and paperback books. I picked up a hardcover book titled, *Washington*. Friends had given it to us when we moved from Washington State. As I opened the cover I noticed the writing. Several friends had wished us luck on our travels and with our new home, and they asked us to stay in touch. I turned a few pages and recognized Puget Sound, where we had fished on the boat many times, and the Flying Fish Market in Seattle, where we stood and watched the fishmongers toss fish. I smiled through the tears.

A large room just off the basement contained yard tools: rakes, shovels, post-hole diggers, tampers, a hedge trimmer, a weed eater, and various other items. We used these tools frequently – dug holes for a new tree or bush, raked the fall leaves, or trimmed the gardens and grass.

I stared at a shovel, and then picked it up and remembered that several years ago, in a different house, Chad and I were lying in bed one night when we were awakened by a strong skunk stench that flowed in through our open bedroom windows. Chad jumped out of bed thinking the dog had tangled with a skunk, or worse, had brought it into the house. He finally found the dog under the bed and I snickered as Chad pressed his face into the spine of the dog. "No smell," he replied. He was lucky there was no smell, because now it could be all over Chad's face. I kept the amusement to myself. Chad grabbed a flashlight and went outside to investigate. After several minutes, he rushed back into the house and said, "Found a skunk in the middle of road, it was flat." He asked me to get out of bed to help retrieve the dead skunk and dispose of it in a sealed container, in hopes the smell would dissipate. We gathered our tools, a trash bag and "shovel," and drowsily stumbled our way to the road in front of the house. Chad aimlessly wandered around in the road; the skunk had disappeared. He said, "There was no way that flat skunk got up and walked away."

My response, "Someone must have driven by and saw it was injured – they stopped, picked it up, and put in their car to take to the vet."

He was so amused by my half-conscious response he stopped in his tracks... his loud outburst of laughter could have woken the neighbors.

Chad was a "stretch-the-truth-a-little" storyteller. Standing there, it occurred to me that every family member, friend, and person he worked with must have heard some variation of that story, and maybe more than once. I didn't mind. Everyone would have had a good laugh and laughter was good for the soul. I laughed to myself as I placed the shovel back where I found it.

The basement was overwhelming and difficult to walk through. Some of Chad's things brought me comfort, but others were painful reminders of his absence in the house. The only thing more painful than looking at his things was the thought of them being bagged up and hauled off as trash.

I had to listen to my heart and carefully sort through every piece. My boundaries were set. I would only work in two-hour segments and then I had to take a break, and would focus on one task at a time. Some days I ran on pure adrenaline. David would say, "You are like a machine." Other days I had no motivation or energy, as if I were paralyzed. There were days I plowed through stuff and when my two-hour timer went off, I would praise my efforts, "Great job Leah." In front of me were three bags for donation, one box of carefully packed crystal wine classes we received as a wedding gift, a pile to sell, and items to give to family.

Many of Chad's items held a memory or a sequence of events. I needed to have the confidence that the things I gave away of Chad's would give the recipient joy, happiness, memories, a big fish, or another story to tell.

Deep inside I felt that it might be disrespectful of Chad's things to give them away. Shouldn't I hold on to them forever? I knew I wouldn't use them. Chad would want his belongings to bring happiness to a fellow sportsman or woodworker. Letting go of these items didn't mean I was letting go of Chad or the emotional energy, it was about moving on. The memories would always remain alive in my heart and I didn't need his things as a reminder.

I knew this would be emotionally and physically draining, but I had to make decisions on everything in that basement — keep it, throw it away, save it for family, garage sale, or donate to charity? Eventually I would learn to let go of all of it, one day at a time.

Chapter 18

TWO WEDDINGS AND MORE CRYING

August was just around the corner and that meant a wedding. My best friend Lynne's daughter was getting married and I was very nervous about going. Weddings, as you know, are such a deep, loving, and strongly emotional time for me, but I needed to continue to face these types of situations head on.

When I arrived on Conomo Point for the big weekend, I was greeted like part of the family, which I always felt that I was. Lynne and I had known each other for what seemed like a lifetime. We were as close as two loving sisters. We vented about work, supported each other through family crises, took vacations together, and often laughed until we cried.

Conomo is a picturesque summer oceanfront community in Massachusetts that's over a hundred years old and has approximately one hundred seasonal cottages and year-round homes. The family stayed in several different houses on the Point. I bunked with Lynne's mom and brother, and his family. Each evening we would sit on one of the oceanfront wrap-around porches and watch the sky, ablaze with fiery orange and searing red as the sun lowered into the shimmering ocean waters. It was like a contest for a few of us to see who could take the best sunset picture. We would pretend to fight, "No mine is better, no MINE is!" It was a significant reminder of the many times Chad and I watched the sunset over the water, and the fun we had together. My heart ached wishing he were there, sharing this time.

At the house, I kept myself occupied with busy work – washing dishes, being a cooking assistant, running errands, and setting up for the festivities. In doing this I didn't have to think or feel, at least in public. Lynne was consciously aware of my feelings, and very sensitive to anything she thought would stir my emotions. But I was also tuned into her feelings with the stress of the day, preparations, entertainment, and family drama. We knew when to gently pull the other aside and say, "Let's go for a walk."

The wedding party arrived, and the following morning an assembly line of twelve women descended on a nail salon for manicures and pedicures. It was enjoyable to see the closeness between family and friends as we checked on each other, complimented our color choices, patiently waited for our turn, chatted, and laughed. The love and positive energy that consumed this room was uplifting and warmed my heart. Female friends provide a support network unlike any other type of friendship. I didn't know all these ladies, but I drew support in the excitement. It made me happy.

The next morning, the wedding day, the same twelve women took over another salon... this time to get hair and makeup done. It was another wonderful experience with the childlike energy that blossomed in each of us. Some elected fancy braids, others straightening, and others a few bouncy curls. I decided to do my own hair; with my frizz and curls most stylists make a fuzzy mess, which is not a good look for me.

The makeup artist was exceptionally talented and quick. She applied makeup sparingly to enhance our features and then sprayed our face with a product that kept our makeup fresh all day, including the lipstick. After my makeup was applied, I picked up a magazine, sat down, and patiently waited on everyone else. Suddenly music blared from speakers in the ceiling, a song by The Dixie Cups. "Going to the chapel and we're gonna get married. Going to the chapel and we're gonna get married. Going to the chapel of love." My eyes immediately filled with tears. The song hit an emotional chord. Lynne rushed over to me and handed me a tissue and waved a magazine in my face to dry the tears. I was overwhelmed and had to step outside. Removing myself from the salon and the music helped me to control my feelings, or was I just suppressing them? This was Meghan's day and I was not going to allow myself to have a negative impact. Deep down I was an emotional mess. The song reminded me of my own wedding and the dreams and plans we had, which would never be.

Later that afternoon we arrived at the beautiful seaside golf course at Bass Rocks Golf Club in Gloucester, Massachusetts – thirty-five miles north of Boston. The sky was a deep blue with a few wispy white clouds; the wedding would take place on the lush lawn overlooking the breathtaking golf course and the Atlantic Ocean. My anxiety was high as I sat in the front row, and I looked around for an escape route, in case I needed it. My intuition was that I would be a crying mess. At the last minute, Meghan asked me to help space the wedding party as they walked down the aisle. I was honored and relieved. Now that I was in the back and had a job, my emotions were much more contained.

The music began and I slowly counted to five between each couple before allowing them to start down the aisle. I quietly reminded them to walk slowly... relax... smile. As the last couple walked by, I turned to see the gorgeous bride and her father standing only feet away. Tears crept in. It reminded me briefly of the love gaze as Chad and I stared into each other's eyes, creating a feeling of deep passion. My heart skipped a beat. The solo guitarist began to play and I gave the bride a big smile and a "thumbs up" as she and her father passed by me. I watched from a distance as Meghan and Devin exchanged vows. This was a much better place for me. I couldn't really hear so I just stared at the backs of the guests' heads – tall ones, short ones, blond hair, dark hair, grey hair, and watched the breeze gently rustle the leaves on the trees. It kept my mind occupied.

There were mostly empty seats at the reception because everyone was jammed on the dance floor. I couldn't help noticing the happy couples... Lynne and Bob, Mary and Bill, Lisa and Tom, Anne and Steve, Margaret and Bobby, and the bride and groom. This was my first large social event without Chad. It was awkward and I felt out of place. Chad was not sitting next to me, dancing with me or chatting with me. There were other single people, not just me... Marilyn, Annie, and Joan... all widows. In the past, I had never noticed if people were alone, but it was becoming more of a focal point for me, particularly in a crowd.

When dining out, I noticed people and wondered if they were on business, was their significant other out of town, were they on a lunch/dinner break from work, maybe single or they lost their spouse? You never know what someone else has been through, but I would always speculate. As I looked around the packed clubhouse that evening, I was happy to be there and honored to be a part of this special day.

Weeks later, I attended another wedding – my nephew, Witt's. I was again nervous.

The elegant wedding took place at the historic Hotel du Pont in Wilmington, Delaware. This twelve-story Italian Renaissance hotel occupied an entire city block and showcased carved woodwork, handcrafted chandeliers, elaborate marble and mosaic floors, original artwork by the Wyeths, and gilded hallways.

Just before the ceremony, family pictures were taken off the lobby area of this magnificent hotel. Each family unit was summoned to stand in front of an enormous fireplace to have their photograph taken. My family unit was just me now, which made me sensitive to the situation. I kept leaving the area and walking around the lobby so I wouldn't have to think about it or see it. Eventually my sister-in-law asked me to join her and her mother, my mother-in-law, in a couple of pictures. It was nice that she did that, but it wasn't the same. Donna, another sister-in-law, asked me to have my picture taken with her, while her husband, Chad's older brother Todd, took our picture at every opportunity in the hotel lobby. It was my impression that Donna felt my uneasiness, and her actions were a welcomed distraction.

The Federal-style du Barry room was stunning, with an exquisite crystal chandelier that was imported from Yugoslavia. It hung from the middle of the fourteen-foot ceiling. Chairs were carefully placed on each side of the room with an aisle that split them down the middle. The mass of friends and family started to stroll down the aisle to take their seats for the ceremony. I buried myself somewhere in the middle of the aisle, close to family. As the room filled, the sound of chatter continued to rise, but silence was drawn when the music began.

I don't remember much about the ceremony, my mind was swimming with my own wedding memories, like Chad and I exchanging vows. We were floating on a cloud of happiness that day. Becoming Mrs. Chad Goodman was the best thing that ever happened to me. Finally, I pulled myself back into the moment... it seemed as if Witt and Ryan's voices were muted. What did I miss while I was reminiscing? After the brief ceremony, everyone was anxious to make their way down the hall to the reception.

Witt and Ryan welcomed their guests into the Gold Ballroom, which was filled with glittering chandeliers, gold rosettes, and bas-reliefs of several famous women. I was seated at a table with family, which was a relief. I didn't want to make small talk with people I didn't know as I was still a bit shy about verbally expressing my new life. Those conversations generally started off with, "Where do you work, do you have kids, are you married?" I wasn't ready for those questions and answers, without displaying some outward emotional distress. The last thing I needed was to cry at my nephew's reception because someone asked me a question. So, I avoided those situations and stayed close to people I knew. The reception began with Witt singing a song he wrote for Ryan, the love of his life.

Later in the evening everyone was on the dance floor – young nieces, tween nephews, and Chad's ninety-one-year-old aunt. The kids were sweaty and some decided to strip off their jackets, ties, and shoes... they were the most fun to watch. The energy and laughter warmed my heart. Allowing myself to enjoy and be open to pleasures in life would create new pathways. I had to learn that this would give me greater perspective on what could be.

Attending the two weddings was a turning point for me. I realized, more than ever, that life is about experiences and sharing those experiences with those you love and care about. I was grateful for the conversations I had, the people I had not seen in a while, and the love that surrounded each and every person. But I was most grateful for the chance to have loved Chad and be loved by Chad, and being enveloped by his family was the next best thing.

With continued support from my therapist, I felt as if I was growing. My ability to value the present moment was stronger than ever, something I was not tuned into before Chad's death.

Chapter 19

LETTING GO

The feeling that Chad would return to his home and to me now faded with each passing day. Embracing the truth was a challenge... one day I was good, the next day not so much. From the beginning, when we are born, people and things come in and out of our lives, and most times we get to choose if the people or things stay or go. We donate toys to Goodwill, dump a mean friend, bequeath a treasured belonging because we know someone needs it more, or give away our out-of-style clothing because we know someone needs it more. Chad was gone from this Earth. He was a precious being, someone I would have never given away or dumped. To have him ripped from my life, and our physical connection completely severed, was unimaginable. How would I live the rest of my life with this?

Grief can be a challenge to manage within a work environment, but Chad's employer was compassionate and supportive of his staff. One thing they did was leave Chad's office untouched. They, too, had trouble letting go. Chad's employer was near and dear to his heart, as were his employees. Chad took great pride in where he worked and gave everyone his utmost respect.

He started his career in Human Resources and worked in that department for ten years before being promoted to Vice President of Nursing. No matter which department Chad was in, he and the staff always had some form of fun during their workweek.

When Chad returned to work after his trip to South Africa, his staff had decorated his office in a jungle theme complete with paper trees, rubber snakes, and stuffed animals. And there was the three-foot-tall trophy that was awarded to someone in the department for some silly reason.

Fridays were dress-down day and Chad frequently took some homemade dessert or bought donuts on his way to work. Staff, residents, and board members were very accommodating during Chad's illness and I felt a strong desire to donate items to the facility and/or certain people, out of respect for Chad.

Chad took many amazing pictures while in South Africa. I picked two and had them enlarged and framed. They're on display in the Human Resource department. I gave Chad's office pictures, mostly of his adventures around the world, to staff he was close to. Some requested a small item from his desk... a pencil holder, picture holder, or knickknack. People were appreciative to receive a small remembrance of Chad, and it brought me great satisfaction to give his belongings to people who mattered to him. I wanted them to look at the item and think of some story he told, his laugh, a look on his face, or a discussion they once had with him. I never wanted him to be forgotten... he was too special to so many people.

In 1996, three years after moving to Syracuse, Chad and I bought a beagle puppy. He was the cutest dog, with his white speckled droopy ears and the most irresistible brown eyes. We named him Donner and he ruled our home for six years, until his death. Chad and I adored him. We took him for walks in the rain and the snow; Chad even took him to work on occasion. Both of us were crushed beyond belief at the loss of our precious dog.

Donner's cremated remains were enclosed in darkness, in a beautiful black tin can with various colors of hand-painted flowers on the exterior. The can always sat on the nightstand, next to my side of bed, with Donner's collar and his framed picture. I was never emotionally able to do anything with his ashes. It was as if I was giving him away. But now I felt differently. I was learning to let go of the physical things and hold on to the memories, which would live forever in my heart.

Donner loved his walks in Clay Park, where we would let him off the leash. He pressed his nose to the ground, sniffed, and followed the scent, but he always returned to us when we called. One beautiful fall afternoon I gave Donner his last ride to the park, where I pulled the lid off the tin can for the first time in over ten years. Tears streamed down my face as I ripped open the small plastic bag. Images flashed through my mind of Chad and I holding hands as we walked Donner on a sunny afternoon, much like this one. I walked to one of Donner's favorite spots on the trail, pushed my right hand into the tin of ashes, and pulled out a handful. As the gentle breeze swept the dust from my hand, tears continued to roll down my face and I watched the remains of my beloved dog float to the ground around me.

Another favorite area was an open green space, where the last bit of ashes sank to the earth. This is where it all started: Donner as a young pup... it's where we trained him to come. Donner was set free in his favorite park, on the trails he so loved and where he would remain forever.

I hoped Donner and Chad found each other and were enjoying walks without me. Life was so different now. No Chad, no Donner, and my life in Syracuse was coming to an end. I was letting go of some of my most treasured things.

Maybe it freed my mind and emotions so I could live with purpose rather than falling into an imagined comfort while suffocating in my "stuff."

The day came when I removed my wedding band and engagement ring. The reminder was too painful, what was and will never be again. Almost daily I opened the box that contained Chad's ashes, but this day Chad's gold wedding band caught my attention. It lay in the tray, under the lid, with his picture looking at me. I picked up the band and rolled it between my fingers... it was bent, scratched, and worn; he never took it off. I looked up at Chad's picture and it was as if he were trying to tell me something. Then an idea popped into my head... to take our two bands and have them melted down into one. What an amazingly sentimental piece of everyday jewelry.

This idea excited me. I immediately called a local jeweler and made an appointment. One week later, I eagerly stood at the jewelry counter and again rolled the ring between my fingers. I could see the engraving on the inside, "Chad & Leah 09/18/92," our wedding day. As my eyes welled with tears I slipped the band on my right ring finger, and smiled. The symbols of love we exchanged years ago were transformed, just as I needed to transform myself and my life.

Over the years, I had accumulated thousands of photos that I kept in three large plastic bins, which I now carried up from the basement and placed in the living room. The task of weeding out bad shots, throwing away duplicates, and organizing the rest was frightening. Was I ready to dive headfirst into Chad's smile, his body, his presence... all on paper?

I stared at the bins, trying to decide which one to open first. I eventually pulled the lid off one and took a handful, they were still in paper envelopes with negatives. I smiled as I looked at Chad in a canoe with a fishing pole. I rubbed my hand across his face, wanting to feel the bearded stubble, but nothing. Tears dripped onto the picture and I gently wiped it off... a wet streak was left across the glossy print.

It took weeks, but with patience, compassion, and strength, I took the lid off each bin and waded through every picture and experienced every emotion known to man. I wept as I thumbed through our wedding photos, smiled as I looked at us holding hands on a walk, chuckled at us wearing sombreros at an office Christmas party. I adored our pictures together no matter the occasion. I was happy to see him smile and delighted with all the family photos. Each picture brought deep thought, trying to pluck from my memory every moment that surrounded that day. I would touch Chad's face, trying to feel his chin or cheek. Looking into his grey eyes, I wished to hear his strong voice and his full-bodied laugh. I longed for his warm embrace as I touched his tiny sleek paper hands. The pain was still there, but not as severe. My heart still ached, but not every second of the day.

Around the house I found myself listening to country music, Chad's favorite. Prior to his death, I listened to almost anything but country music. I was learning that the country music of today was very different from the country music of my childhood, which I found depressing. Someone always lost a love, had a cheating lover, cried in their beer, fell apart, was in prison, or stayed drunk... and I didn't need to be more saddened. Today's country music was more upbeat and energizing, and it put my body in a feel-good mood – cruising, friends, liking it, loving it, good times, chillin', a great day, fun life, better life, happiest girl, beauty, and heaven. I felt I had been missing out all these years, but it also made me feel closer to Chad, doing something that he enjoyed.

We often played board games with our godson, family, and friends, and had two shelves worth of games in the hallway closet. Chad's favorite was Aggravation – a board with many holes and you worked your four same-color marbles around the board to home via a dice roll. Chad used to say, "This game aggravates me." We would all laugh, but continued to play one game after another. Sometimes Chad would agree to play, but deep down I don't think he enjoyed these games all that much. He would grumble a little about playing, but once we started he would become competitive and humorous. It's times like these I hold close to my heart, times like these that make me smile. The joy was beginning to overshadow the heartache.

I had numerous garage sales and many friends and co-workers wanted a heads-up before I opened them to the public. Our friends, John and MaryAnn, wanted to buy our beer glasses. When they took them they had distressed looks on their faces... no smiles, just tears in their eyes. They loved their beer and said, "We'll think of you and Chad every time we use them." That gave me such a sense of honor, knowing they would do exactly that.

Another friend wanted to buy a beautiful, tall, media chest with ten small doors that was on display in our living room. She wanted it for her husband's office so he could remember his friend Chad. Many friends seemed to attach themselves to something that had a certain meaning to them, and that was my goal. However, not everything could go to someone we knew.

One morning before the garage sale opened, a man arrived and wanted to see the three large cabinets I advertised. I escorted him down into the basement so he could take a look, and he bought them on the spot. He knew from looking at the basement that a man lived there, or used to. On our way upstairs he made an insensitive comment, "I know what you're doing. You and your husband are getting divorced and you're selling his stuff." My chest tightened. I wanted to cry but didn't. I could only wish Chad was still alive. I glared into his eyes; he didn't deserve a response. Some people were also very nosy. "Are you moving, and why are you moving. Are you married?" I don't like sharing such personal information with strangers, so I would just change the subject.

At the very first garage sale I befriended a middle-aged woman and her young married daughter. They were on a tight budget and were looking for deals. I gave them many such deals, which I was pleased to do. Helping people in need was something I felt good about. The last time I saw them, they had a van full of our household items, purchased for only a few dollars. The sight brought out a cheerful smile.

Letting go of my, his, our stuff seemed to strengthen my will, making the harder decisions somewhat easier. I became more and more selective in what to keep, but sometimes I kept something and later decided I didn't need it. The mental shift into another stage of my life became clearer and it did no good to cling to the stuff. The emotional attachment immobilized my healing and would prevent me from moving on. Every item I saved had to be cleaned, repaired, or maintained over its lifetime, and I decided to sacrifice "stuff" in the pursuit of a simpler life.

Chapter 20

LEAVING MY LIFE IN THE REARVIEW MIRROR

It took me many months and lots of hard work to reach this day, the day I left Syracuse. The best years of my life were lived here, but so were the worst.

Cindi reminded me: "The previous chapters in your life have already been written. You are beginning a new chapter and you are responsible for writing it."

Something else that stuck with me... going into the second year of the death of a spouse was referred to as "the year of change." I never considered myself to be a follower, but in this instance, I was comforted by the fact that I was doing something that was considered "normal." It validated my decision.

My mind whirled as I stepped into our shower for the last time. My body was numb as the water rushed down over my head, thinking of the upcoming hours... the last time I used our bathroom, the last time I slept in our bed, the last walk around the house, the last time in our house. I concluded that the spirit of our home would always be with me, in my heart, deeply rooted in my soul, forever. I'm not sure how long I was in the shower, but I used every drop of hot water. As hard as it was, it was time for me to go. My life here was done.

My SUV was loaded, packed with my suitcases and several boxes I was leaving in storage at my mom's. I walked around the almost-empty house and etched memories into my brain... the parties we hosted, the sunroom where we cuddled and watched the snow fall, the nights we embraced each other in front of the roaring fireplace while we watched a movie, and our evening dinners sitting at the kitchen bar. As tears trickled down my cheeks, I turned down the thermostat, turned off the water valve, and lowered the temperature of the hot water tank. All things Chad taught me to do before we left the house on vacation. The finality of leaving my home was overwhelming. With tears now streaming down my face, I sat on the kitchen floor with my back against a cabinet. I pulled my knees into my chest and wrapped my arms around them, staring at the ceiling. "I'm sorry, Chad, I just can't live here anymore."

I was not going to allow this life to beat me up anymore. I took one quick look around, made sure the doors and windows were locked and the curtains and shades were pulled, then I set the security system and closed the door behind me. I didn't think, I just did... one foot in front of the other. I climbed into my car, drove out of the garage, and never looked back. It was surreal, like I was watching myself go through the motions and not believing they were happening.

It was a cool November morning and the sun shone brightly in the brilliant blue sky. As I merged onto the highway, my grief, guilt, and fear of the future seemed to lighten. It was a good feeling. I drove south through the City of Syracuse.

On the left was the medical complex where Chad took his last breath, and on the right was the tall office building where I last worked, on the fifteen floor. A tingling sensation moved through my shoulders and arms, and numbness moved into my hands. I briefly let go of the steering wheel and shook both hands from the wrist. Since Chad's death seventeen months ago, I had ridden in the front seat of a wild and crazy emotional rollercoaster and I was ready for the ride to level out. I hoped to make this happen by focusing on positive changes and new adventures.

The first step in my new life outside of Syracuse was to visit Chad's family, followed by a drive to my family, and a subsequent trek across the country to Long Beach, California, where I would leave my car to be shipped to the Island of Hawaii. My mom told me several times that the trip sounded exhausting, but I reminded her that it was part of my journey.

There were many conversations with myself on the four-hour drive. What was I doing? I was moving on, right? A new chapter in my life in a new location, and what better place than the tropics? Was I really doing this? What does my family really think? What does it matter, right? Now it's not about them, it's about me. They will come and visit, hopefully. And, I will visit them.

Eventually, I turned the radio on to drown out my thoughts.

The Goodmans always came together when I visited. We enjoyed evening dinners, competitive board games, the latest action adventure movie, or a local event. My pleasure was watching my nieces and nephews play soccer, practice karate, ride horses, play the violin and flute, and dance and sing. Everyone wanted me to do and see everything with them, which gave me a sense of love and of being needed.

My nephew David had just celebrated his twelfth birthday and received a tree house, with a swing that dropped what seemed like fifty feet out of a tree, but it was probably more like fifteen feet. He couldn't wait for me to try it and continued to beg me to jump with him. My reply was, "In a few minutes," as I kept talking to the adults. In reality, I was afraid. I never liked the free-falling feeling and this activity scared me. He continued to beg and I finally said, "Yes!" I couldn't let my nephew know I was afraid, because he looked up to me. After all, I had spent years in the United States Army; he thought I was tough.

David scaled the ladder in seconds and I followed leisurely behind. He went first and showed me precisely what I needed to do. I watched carefully as he jumped without hesitation and swung back and forth until he jumped off and landed on his feet on the ground.

He yelled up to me, "It's easy, Aunt Leah!"

Under my breath I replied, "For YOU, yes it is."

With my stomach in my throat, I tightly grabbed the rope and slowly moved to the edge of the platform and looked down. What was I about to do? My heart raced as I closed my eyes and took the leap into thin air. I released my anxiety with a loud scream, and with my fingers firmly wrapped around the rope I swung back and forth through the trees, feeling weightless. There was a fluttering sensation in my stomach.

Fear is an illusion and I created it in my mind. But I didn't let my fear of jumping prevent me from having an amazing experience with my nephew. I only postponed it by blowing him off several times, hoping he would forget. But I learned something… it was not as bad as I feared. Actually, it was a lot of fun. If I continued to allow my fears to dictate my actions, I would go nowhere.

I thought of one of my favorite books, *A Year of Miracles,* by Marianne Williamson. I should guide my thinking to thoughts of love; it will help break the chains of fear that bind me. Working miracles starts inside me and my mind. I sometimes put limits or constraints on myself. Why? Because I'm afraid? What else was I missing out on?

The Goodmans got together one evening for dinner; the adults gathered in the dining room, while the kids played in the basement. I pictured Chad sitting near the food, devouring the Fritos and clam dip his mother was famous for making. He would always be in the middle of some debate on politics or healthcare, and he took great pleasure in giving someone a hard time. He loved stealing Anna and Amy's noses, but would always put them back in the correct spot on their faces. Brooke loved to snuggle with her uncle and he would often pretend to put on her small jacket, hat, or shoes. Daniel and David would listen for hours as Chad told stories or showed them karate moves.

Just before dinner I opened two bottles of champagne Chad and I received on our wedding day. Yes, I had kept them for twenty years. We toasted to life, health, love, and happiness. I felt deeply saddened because Chad was missing, that evening, from the laughs, the stories, the family time together, and most of all, the nieces and nephews.

I made one last trip into his mom's finished basement where I left Chad's ashes, for now. His mother had set up a small shrine on top of the piano with pictures, knickknacks, and mementos. I slowly opened the lid and smiled at his picture on the inside, he looked so happy. Chad was at peace now, but that thought didn't prevent me from missing him. I ran my fingers across the picture and then blew him a kiss as I closed the lid. How would I ever learn to live without him?

As I pulled out of my mother-in-law's driveway, I felt that a vital chunk of me was being left behind, like an incomplete jigsaw puzzle. I hoped to fill my empty space someday and be whole again. Leaving Chad's family did not mean the end of the relationship, but it would change it. Moving thousands of miles away would no longer mean an easy weekend drive. There was an excited closeness with Chad's family, which gave me a warm, loving feeling. I felt needed. A concern suddenly swept through my mind... will they forget me? A few miles on the highway I pulled over; I could barely see through the tears that were gushing down my face.

Several hours and 574 miles later, I happily arrived at my mom's. She welcomed me with a smile and open arms. When I was a child I would get into my mom's closet and try on her various high-heeled shoes. Mom was cool and I wanted to be just like her. Then at about age sixteen, mom became not so cool. She told me what to do, how do it, and when to do it... she was no fun. Of course, I knew everything and she knew nothing. It wasn't until years later that I learned to appreciate her ways. She only wanted the best for me growing up, and still did.

Getting together with my brother and his family was always an exciting time. Jenna and Jonathan, both teenagers, loved to tell stories, particularly funny stories about school, their friends, their mom and dad, or each other. It was an entertaining evening of listening and laughing. Chad was fond of spending time with both of them, especially the fishing trips with Jonathan, teasing him about eating possum pizza, and the lemon-eating contest. Jenna and Chad took pleasure in performing stunts in the pool, boogie boarding in Myrtle Beach, and riding the biggest, fastest roller coasters.

I don't see much of my brother. He works many hours a day, at least six days a week, and never seems to have time.

What's with our society? Everyone seems to work too much, be stressed out, and have little to no time for family, let alone a vacation. I hoped my family and friends learned something from Chad's death. But maybe they weren't supposed to?

It smacked me hard across the face... I have a limited number of days on this earth and I want to spend my time enjoying it today, not tomorrow. Some people put things off until it's too late, then it's no longer an option. The guilt and regret will eventually add to the burden of grief, which can make the healing process much more difficult. Are they really living life? Or are they in survival mode? What are they not getting? Or is it me? What am I missing?

It was Thanksgiving Day. Mom and I dined at Jenny Wiley State Resort Park Restaurant, which is nestled among soaring pine trees and peaceful mountains, overlooking a sprawling lake. As we approached the front door, I saw that the long entryway was decorated with large colorful pumpkins, bales of dry hay, and gathered corn stalks. As I opened the front door, the aroma of savory and sweet smacked me in the face. The hostess greeted us with a smile and seated us near the window, looking out over the lake. Surrounding tables were filled with people laughing and chatting.

This is my life now... admiring the togetherness of other families enjoying a holiday meal. How did this happen? Family Thanksgiving dinners as a kid, to large Thanksgiving dinners with Chad's big family, to just Mom and me? I was grateful to spend the day, share a meal, and give thanks with her, but I longed to have every person I loved at that lakefront table that day.

It was a tearful good-bye to my family, but something I knew I had to do. Moving away from everyone was a detour I needed to take. Leaving my family and friends would only make me stronger and give me the ability to offer more to myself and others than I could ever imagine.

Chapter 21

THE REFLECTIVE DRIVE

I hopped on the Bert T. Combs Mountain Parkway, a curvy two and four-lane rural state highway, which runs from the mountainous Appalachian region of Eastern Kentucky through the rolling tobacco fields of Central Kentucky. It took me almost to Lexington, where I picked up I-70 West.

The drive through the Bluegrass State was uneventful, mostly flat terrain and gloomy skies, but I was mesmerized by the infinite yellow line in the middle of the road. This was my road to better things... rebuilding my life and growing in a new direction. Looking towards the future. But a part of me felt disloyal – getting rid of Chad's things, moving away from our life together, and leaving his ashes at his mom's. I needed to live my life, which would continue to happen, and it would hurt, bring happiness and sorrow, and I would heal the damage and move on, writing those chapters of my life, one at a time.

As I approached St. Louis, Missouri, I noticed a sign, "O'Fallon, Illinois," where my brother was born, and I went from kindergarten through second grade. I yearned to see my old house and old neighborhood and remember those untroubled days. I took the exit and pulled into the nearest gas station, where I entered my former street address into the GPS. I was excited but nervous as I drove the four miles. What would I remember? Did neighbors still live there?

I approached the railroad track crossing at the entrance of the housing development, remembering standing there as a child, holding my father's hand as a train car slowly chugged by with an American Flag draped down one side. Many people lined the tracks at that moment and quietly watched the train until it disappeared. The year was 1968 and my dad told me the train carried the body of Robert F. Kennedy, who had just been assassinated.

My mind flashed to Chad… he was about the same age as RFK when he passed away. The realization of not knowing when, where, or how death would come frightened me; I broke out into a hot, nauseated sweat. I wiped the palms of my hands on my jean-covered thighs as the steering wheel slipped through my hands. I barely made the turn onto Willow Drive.

As I hunched over the steering wheel and slowly drove down the street, I looked for something I recognized. Suddenly our house appeared on the left. I stopped in the middle of the road, my heart pounding harder and faster… the house was much smaller than I remembered, but it was so familiar: a ranch-style home with a bay window in front, shutters on each window, and a single-car garage. Many memories were made there: my brother curled up in the bay window hiding from Mom, learning how to ride my bicycle in the driveway and crashing into the trashcans at the curb, watching my dad shave before he went to work, Mom cooking dinner, my brother "accidently" taking the car out of park and rolling it into the street, holding talent shows for the neighbors in the garage, dad putting too much soap in the new dishwasher leaving knee-deep suds on the kitchen floor. I smiled with tear-filled eyes; those were the carefree days.

Being concerned about Neighborhood Watch, I continued slowly down the street and turned around. My instinct was to stop and take a picture of my house or knock on the door, but I wasn't brave enough to do either. As I turned onto the main road, I felt optimistic. I was happy in that house. My parents were healthy, my family was intact, and I felt loved. I also felt safe from a harsh world that I did not yet realize, at the time, even existed.

I continued on I-70 West across the state of Missouri and remembered the many friends, neighbors, co-workers, and acquaintances throughout my life. People come in and out of our lives for a reason, and most of the time we don't know the why... maybe to teach us a lesson or introduce us to someone. Maybe to become a lifelong friend. These people have various qualities – kind, polite, gentle, sincere, but others can be insensitive, finicky, rude, and stubborn. Although we all exhibit both positive and negative traits, we accept the good and the bad in the ones we love.

When I married Chad, was it his fate to die at an early age? Was I the cause? What if he had married someone else, would the outcome have been the same? What if I had taken a different path in life, or what if he had? What if we had never met? Would he still be alive?

It was 1990. I sat in a church pew awaiting the start of a wedding ceremony when out of the corner of my eye I saw a tall hunk of a muscular man. He was very handsome in his Army dress uniform. His green jacket was buttoned and it displayed numerous badges, ribbons, and a nametag: "Goodman." I gawked at him through the entire ceremony. During the reception, I noticed that Goodman played with the kids and talked to almost everyone, except for me. There was an air of confidence that surrounded him and he seemed calm. I thought about him many times over the next several days. Finally, I talked to the groom and asked, "Who was that good looking best man?" He replied, with a smile, "He's single."

Why was the love of my life taken from me? Why?

Chad loved me more than anything. He accepted my shortcomings and took good-hearted pleasure in sometimes poking fun at them. When we went to a party, he was by my side. We could agree to disagree. He attempted to cook... once in a while. We had fights and yelled and didn't talk to each other for hours, but we got over it. He let me decorate our home with little to no input, and slept in our pink bedroom for several years with no complaints. When I said I wanted a coat tree for our entryway, he made me one. Occasionally he would call me at work just to say, "I love you." I had no doubt he loved me.

Why was he taken from me? We had plans. He had plans.

When we retired, we were going to buy an RV and travel the United States. Our short list: hike in Acadia, the Grand Canyon, and Yellowstone; fish in Montana, Washington, and Alaska; paddle the rivers of Minnesota, Kentucky, and Georgia. There was so much left to do. Before retirement though, Chad wanted to be president of the company he worked for. He had finished the necessary college courses just before his diagnosis and was awaiting a test date from New York State. He would have been a remarkable president for the large health care facility. But it was not meant to be.

Why was he taken from me? He taught me a lot, but I had more to learn.

Chad taught me many things. He taught me to think things through, be logical, have a sense of humor. Be tough, when you need to be. Root for the underdog. Help those in need. Find good in everyone. Be patient (not that he always was). Teach. Don't expect too much from others. Love thy neighbor. Laugh more. Pursue your passion. Be good at what you choose to do. Enjoy life. Listen more. There's a beginning and an end. Accept death. Move on.

If I hadn't learned all these things from Chad, would he still be here with me? Was there one thing I learned from him that was his death sentence? Do we have a to-do list in this life and when that's complete we fade to dust and move to the afterlife? I still have more to learn, and who will teach me now?

I flipped back to the happy, fun, and innocent times of my childhood. As a preschooler, I wanted my hair in cornrows, because my friend Cookie had them. I rode my bright red pedal car in the basement, but only if someone was with me. I was afraid to be down there alone. I recalled the frilly dresses, floppy hats, and patent leather shoes my mom made me wear to play outside. The many road trips we took as a family, with my brother and me in the back seat and no seat belt or car seat. The times I complained to my mom about my brother, "He's looking at me!" I used to stand on the hump in the back floorboard, place my little arms on the top of the front bench seat between my parents, and sing for hours.

One long car trip, in particular, I learned how to tie my shoes by using the "Fisher Price Music Box Lacing Shoe." It was a large plastic and wood shoe on wheels that looked like a house. It played the nursery rhyme, *There Was an Old Woman That Lived in a Shoe*, as scenes popped up in the windows. It took me hours, but with determination I tied the shoe over and over again until I mastered the art.

A nice tall lady who lived across the street and drove a cool car allowed me to pick pansies from her flower garden, because they were my favorite.

It finally registered… happiness is not the absence of problems, because we all have them, but our ability to deal with them. In that moment, I chose to remember the blessings in my young life.

Now I was scared to death about my future, but forced myself to take the next step. Much like the tree house swing, it might be fun. Just because life has its rough stretches doesn't mean I can't laugh and be happy and enjoy the things around me.

As nightfall approached, I stopped for gas in Kansas City and there was a Best Western across the street. My mind had been racing for several hours and I was exhausted from talking to myself. As the hotel attendant handed me the keys, he said, "You traveling alone?" Here we go again, what's with the questions from strangers? I grabbed my overnight bag and walked toward the elevator. Are people really that nosy? Concerned that I'm alone? Or hitting on me? I did not have the energy or the time to give away right now. Was I turning into an unfriendly being? I hoped not.

The next morning, I continued the drive across Kansas, which was flat and boring and seemed to last forever. Farmlands and rolling hills hugged the highway from east to west, with exits few and far between. Radio stations did not seem to last for more than a few miles, so I switched the radio off. My mind wandered... what do people think when they open their mouth sometimes?

"You are lucky, Leah!"

You consider me lucky? Watching my strong husband whittle away to nothing, you call that lucky? Losing the love of my life, you call that lucky?

"I wish I had your life, Leah!"

I'll trade you for one day, guaranteed you will want to trade back.

"I'm jealous, Leah!"

Jealous of what? Are you kidding me? You want my pain?

The razor-sharp point of a knife piercing your chest as the blood flows down your body and pools on the ground beneath you, and you feel like you're going to die as your

137

chest cavity is split open and your heart ripped out, sliced into thousands of tiny pieces... sobbing as you frantically try to put it back together, make the bleeding stop... make the agonizing pain go away.

You still think I'm lucky? Are you still jealous?

"Why are you moving away, Leah? You are moving so far away, Leah! You are moving away from family and friends, Leah? You are retiring, Leah? You are too young to retire!"

Really, what age do I need to be?

"You are so lucky, Leah!"

The top of my head was about to explode. Some people glorified Chad's death; it felt as if I was the first one to cross the finish line as the black and white checkered flags dropped and I was declared the winner. Where's my trophy... oh yeah, you can't see it, it's the huge hole in my heart. It's not the kind of trophy you can display on the shelf for everyone to ooh and aah over. Just because I choose to wear a beautiful happy smile, don't assume it's not without struggle.

Chad gave me many gifts, and I'm truly grateful. One lesson I'm most grateful for – Chad was adamant that we pay into our retirement plan first, and then live off what was left. That was our choice, to plan for our future. Before Chad, I lived paycheck to paycheck... stashing very little into savings.

Crossing the border of Kansas into Colorado was not much of a change in scenery... wide open plains lined the roadway. I only had another 180 miles or so to reach Fern's house, Chad's cousin. Two full days of driving and living in my head; it was time for some distractions.

Once I arrived, Fern and I sat at her kitchen table for hours and shared stories of family, the death of her son, Chad's death, her work, her cat, her loving husband, our relationship, and her love for Denver. She got it. We cried about our losses, laughed at life, and had serious chats about family.

One afternoon, Fern took me to one of her favorite spots – the Denver Botanic Gardens, which was nestled in a quiet neighborhood not far from her home. It was a typical mild winter day, sunny and mid-40's. We walked many of the outdoor paths through the vast array of sculptures, water features, and gazebos. Each plant was labeled and even though most were dead or not yet in bloom, the gardens were still stunning. It reminded me of life... we beautifully sprout, grow, and bloom... there are many paths in our lives... then someday, we cease to exist.

The drive west out of Denver was breathtaking. The snow-covered peaks of the Rocky Mountains stretched up into the crystal-clear, dark blue sky. It didn't seem real. It had that fake look as if it were a backdrop for a movie. The grand mountain peaks gradually turned into sprawling desert hills and red sandstone formations. I was mesmerized by the beauty all the way to St. George, Utah. Then came the crazy LA traffic, which was nerve-racking, but my GPS clearly directed me to my hotel in West Hollywood. I carried two large suitcases and a carry-on to my room, where I unpacked and repacked everything and discarded a few items.

The next morning, I made the horrific ten-lane traffic-jammed commute to Long Beach, where I left my car to be shipped to the Island of Hawaii. By leaving the one familiar thing I had, my anxiety level escalated. My insides were jittery and I worried about my car, like it had feelings. It would be alone on a huge ship sailing across the Pacific. What if it sank and I experienced another loss? Was I having separation anxiety? Ten days from now I should be able to pick up my car at the port in Kawaihae. I turned and walked away from my car with tear-filled eyes.

I gazed at a single spot on the ceiling most of the night, tossed and turned while I worried about my car, my life, and my future. What was I doing and where was my life headed? I couldn't believe I had just driven across the country. Everything I experienced over the last few days was foreign;

when would life become normal again? Would it ever be normal? I jumped out of bed before my alarm went off. What was the point of just lying there worrying? For a brief moment, I stared at the only things I had – two large suitcases and a carry-on bag. I took in a deep breath. How did I whittle down a house to three pieces of luggage? I rolled my possessions out the front door of the hotel onto Sunset Boulevard and grabbed a taxi to the Los Angeles International Airport.

As I sat in the back seat and looked out the window, I noticed the sun coming up in the distance... a new day was beginning. The driver pulled up to the departure terminal and dropped me off. As I rolled my luggage inside, I wondered how many other people here were starting over today. The day began in LA with a few million people, but would end in Kona with slightly less than 40,000.

My life was going to be extremely different, more different than anything I had ever known.

Chapter 22

MY NEW HOME

The Big Island of Hawaii is larger than all the other Hawaiian Islands combined. It's immense enough to hold eleven out of thirteen of the world's climate zones – from sunny hot beaches to freezing snowcapped mountaintops. With an area of over 4,000 square miles and spectacular contrasts of black lava fields, lush green forests, snow topped mountains, and 266 miles of coastline, there are a wide variety of activities to explore.

Kona has a calm and easy feel. The residents have the most laid-back attitudes, no road rage or vehicles speeding through a red light. Most drivers actually stop at crosswalks to allow pedestrians to cross the street. The weather is consistent all year, with only two seasons: winter and summer. The average summer temperature is eighty-five degrees, while the average winter temperature is only eight degrees cooler. A pleasant change from the 120 inches of average snow fall in Syracuse, with temperatures in February sometimes in the single digits.

There's something mystical about the Big Island... it calls to people from all over the world. Some believe it's the spiritual energy of this unique place that speaks to them, that allows openness and cultivation of the soul. Others believe it's the spirit of Aloha from the Native Hawaiian people that promotes the forgiveness, love, peace, and understanding that contributes to the magic of the island. Others trust it's the ocean on the Kona side, because it circulates from international waters and there's little river run-off, creating pure salt water for healing.

In the midst of the extraordinary splendor of the island, healing and personal transformation seem to accelerate. That's why the island has long been known as "The Healing Island." This island is also the land of myths and legends, passed down by the people who live here. Legend has it that Royal Hawaiians often visited the island to rest, restore, and rejuvenate their spirit. Another legend suggests that Polynesians traveled thousands of miles over the rough sea to find Hawaii. They were drawn to the spirit of "Lokah," harmony of mind, body, and spirit. Over hundreds of years, Native Hawaiians have taken their traditions and fused them with Eastern and Western ways, to create the renewing energy of their land.

As the plane descended into the Kona Airport, I marveled through the window at the blue ocean and black lava as the Captain announced, "We should be on the ground in ten minutes and the weather in Kona is sunny and 81." Perfect! The flight attendants took their seats just before the wheels made contact with the runway. The engines came to a soft hum as the plane slowed and taxied to the gate. I was truly excited and could hardly wait to debark; I was ready to begin my new life.

As I stepped off the plane, the bright Hawaii sun beamed down onto my smiling face and a gentle breeze swept through my hair. This is now my home, the place I chose to move forward, to heal and reclaim my life. I picked up my rental car and drove to my condo. It had been almost a year since I last saw it, and only seven months since I closed the deal. Would it have the same calm and comfortable feel?

I struggled to park the gargantuan light blue Crown Victoria in a parking spot, cussing under my breath as I backed up and pulled forward several times to get between the lines. People probably thought I was a novice driver. The economy car I had reserved was not available, so this boat on wheels would have to do. At least there was plenty of room for luggage! My struggles didn't end with the car, but continued as I wrestled with two fifty-pound suitcases. I held the top handle as I pulled the weight up one stair rung and then another, until I was on the third floor. By the time all the luggage was outside my condo, my heart was pounding hard. I tried to catch my breath, standing tensely at my new front door. I inserted the key into the knob and slowly swung the door open. Stale air hit me in the face as I moved across the threshold. I walked around and opened the windows and doors, allowing the light and breeze to pour in, along with the soft sounds of ocean waves. There's something so soothing about listening to and watching the ocean. It has the ability to silence the mind, promote calmness within, and provide a sense of wellbeing. The powerful force demands nothing, while freely granting its gift.

A sunset always had the ability to slow me down, and tonight was no different. I stepped out onto the lanai and stared out into miles of open space; I felt connected to life and the world at that moment. It was like an umbilical cord that provided life-enhancing energy. As the sun slowly faded below the horizon, my spirit seemed to shift to another level. There's something out there, but what is it? It was as if my body was injected with rejuvenation and inspiration. Suddenly I felt content. I closed my eyes, took several deep breaths, and focused on the present as the ocean noise filled my head.

It's the simple things in life that mean the most. Although my life was not perfect, there were many things to be grateful for... loving family, amazing friends, my health, and my new home. I'm grateful for the air I breathe, the food I eat, and the sunshine that brightens my every day. I made a promise to myself to not get stuck in the past or obsess over the future... to live in the present as much as possible. It would create a happy life.

Just before bed I walked out onto the lanai again and sat down at the table. I looked up and fixated on a twinkling star. Was this Chad? Did he follow me here? Of course he did. I gently whispered to him "I love you, wish you were here sitting next to me." I wondered what Chad thought of my decisions so far. Was he smiling or scratching his head?

It was a restless sleep, if I slept at all. My sprawled body consumed the king size bed as I tossed and turned most of the night. What have I done? What will I do tomorrow? Is my car okay on the ship? I couldn't settle down enough to slip into that deep unconscious state. My tranquil body never moved when I lay next to Chad; I felt safe, secure, and stable... feelings I continued to battle with.

Chapter 23

MY FIRST "LIFE EXPERIENCE" IN KONA

The scale was beginning to tip the other way... I was not constantly reminded of the painful times. Every morning I woke up in the emptiness of my bed, but I began to think about a new day, going to the gym, or a book I wanted to read. The kick-start into my new life seemed to wash away some of the pain. I was beginning to live life with absolute determination.

One of Chad's gifts to me was being able to live my life more purposefully with love and happiness. He would want me to be happy... not the forced smile, day-to-day survival, only somewhat happy — but rather a deep, centered-in-life happy.

Most mornings I started with a phone call to my mom. I wanted to somehow comfort her, let her know I was okay and not to worry. I told her about my condo previously being a rental and that it was worn and needed lots of TLC. I went over my to-do list with her... paint the ceilings and walls, tear up the linoleum in the kitchen and bathroom and lay tile, tear up the ugly green carpet and lay hardwood floors throughout the rest of the condo, and install a new vanity and toilet in the bathroom. She chuckled and responded, "Good luck with all that."

Painting was something I had experience with and I immediately went into search mode for a paint color. In my numerous trips in and out of the condo complex, I continued to see a couple around my age in the designated smoking area. One morning as I walked my trash to the dumpster, I recognized the couple sitting on a bench. This time I stopped and introduced myself. They were from Arizona and visiting Hawaii for a few months with the husband's teenage son from a former marriage, and he was looking for odd jobs to earn a little cash. I told them I may have a home project or two, but I'd review my list and be in touch. I walked away excited; I might have some help!

After working out the details, Logan arrived at my condo on time, which was rare in Hawaii. If store hours are posted or you hire someone to start at a specific time, you sometimes have to accept an hour or maybe two late… it depends on the surf. Some of the locals like to catch a few waves before the start of their day. I was beginning to understand the low key and no stress of Hawaiian life, and I liked it.

Logan was a tall, slender, eighteen-year-old with a bright smile and blond hair. He had a positive and cheerful attitude, and was respectful, "Excuse me, Leah, thank you, Leah, does this look good, Leah?" I showed him his workspace and the kitchen cabinets I wanted him to sand, prime, and paint. As he pulled out a screwdriver and started to remove the hinges on a cabinet door, I poured my paint into the tray and started with the ceiling in the living room.

When I work, I tend to focus on the job and don't normally participate in idle chitchat. However, this time was different. Logan was an impressionable young man and I wanted to get to know him and make him comfortable working in my home. So, I began to ask questions. He told me about his home in Arizona, his job search, classes to get his GED, home projects with his dad, and Hawaii. All the while, I showed genuine interest in him and his life. My questions stimulated deeper conversations about life, how tough it can be, the uncertainty, the struggles, and the direction we choose. I related to some of his teenage struggles, the confusion that filled his head... should he go to college or learn a trade? And, every adult had conflicting opinions, which added to his frustration. Then there was pressure from friends to drink and do drugs. Just paying attention and listening to Logan seemed to lift his spirits. When I provided some form of encouragement, "You are smart, you'll figure it out," or "I'm proud of you," he seemed motivated to take a step in life and not just talk about it. I wanted to give him hope, and the belief that he could do anything he wanted if he put his mind to it.

Over the course of the next two days we continued to share life stories, but there was one story that yanked on my already damaged heart. Logan's parents divorced when he was six years old and as the years passed, confusion and darkness filled his world, which left a huge hole in his heart much like mine... although he didn't know that about me. His hopes and dreams of family were torn apart. So were mine, but he didn't know that either. During his young teenage years, he was introduced to drugs, sex, and alcohol, which filled his emptiness, or so he thought. By sixteen he was abusing crystal meth and at seventeen he dropped out of high school. Even after he initiated a fight and was left inside an emergency room entrance covered in blood, he continued to abuse drugs. His rock bottom finally came when he overdosed on crystal meth and was extremely close to cardiac arrest. When he recovered, he turned to the only thing left in his life, God. After almost losing his life, Logan was ready to be free of his addictions and begged God to save his life. With the help of his stepmother he went through withdrawal without professional help, and was successful.

I told Logan again and again what a strong person he was. His plan was to eventually return to Arizona and enroll in HVAC (heating, ventilation, air conditioning) school. I carefully listened to every detail as I held back the tears... no child should ever have to suffer such heartache and pain. Why couldn't everyone have a stable and happy childhood, like the one I remembered having?

Logan and I connected. There was a level of trust between us; he shared his personal stories and I shared some of mine. But I never shared my deepest secret... Chad. We seemed to live by some of the same rules – maintain harmony and balance, keep it simple, treasure relationships, and be true to yourself. Logan had his head on straight: he read devotionals every morning, didn't drink, and had a plan. When he gifted me his most recently read book, I was deeply honored and accepted it with gratitude. He said when he finished reading a book that meant something he liked to give it to someone he thought needed it. He was a smart kid, and even though I never discussed my pain, somehow, he knew it was there. This young man touched my heart; he was a fighter and a survivor, with a good soul.

Two months later I learned that Logan had returned to Arizona and relapsed into his old ways. This time he sought professional help through Teen Challenge, an organization that offers transformation to those in need, through Christ-based programs. I was relieved that he sought professional help and I wanted to show my support. Logan could only receive cards and letters, no books or other goodies. I bought six cards of encouragement and vowed to send him one with a note on a regular basis. I could not imagine what he was going through, but I wanted Logan to know I was thinking of him. I was crushed as I remembered how encouraged he was and seemed to have an idea of the productive direction he wanted his life to go. After several weeks of consistently sending a weekly card, I received his first letter. "It blows my mind every time I receive a card or letter from you. The fact that you take the time out of your life to write an eighteen-year-old kid in rehab makes me question how good of a person I am."

Tears rolled down my face, I knew he was a good person – the person who helped me paint my kitchen cabinets, the person who gave me a devotional, the person who had a positive plan when he left Hawaii, the person who, just a few months earlier, believed in himself, respected himself, and others. He was worth my time and energy. I was determined to help him. I was on a mission, and continued to send a weekly card filled with positive messages surrounding his self-worth, positive choices, and investing in his life.

Logan often wrote back, "Thank you, you have an amazing heart." If my minute actions could help him survive, I would do it for it as long as I could. We all deserve love, support, and a chance. Every month I received a letter or post card from Logan that deeply touched me. He expressed how thankful he was for my uplifting notes and the inspiration he found in each and every one. He explained how he looked forward to getting mail, and that he smiled when he returned to his room to find an envelope with my return address. This continued for sixteen months, until Logan graduated from Teen Challenge. My wish was that I gave him hope and helped him to believe in himself again. In the last letter I received from Logan he was doing well and working at Teen Challenge. Every now and then he crosses my mind, and I hope he is living out his dreams.

My motivation to help Logan, by whatever means I could, was driven by a strong emotion. Was my heart healing as I helped a young man? I didn't consider my acts as "going out of my way" or something "I didn't have to do," as he said. For just one moment in his day, I wanted to make him laugh, smile, or think about how much better his life was and could be. For an instant, I wanted to take away his suffering.

Chapter 24

THE SIGNS

I believe in the power of signs. They give me reassurance and hope that Chad is still somehow with me.

Sometimes I search for them because I need them at that moment. Something, anything, a sign from heaven, a sign from Chad. It gives me the impression that he's reaching out to hold my hand, to ease the grief and comfort my heart.

Not long after I moved into my new home, a large black moth appeared on a window screen. Its wingspan was five to six inches from tip to tip and it clung to the upper right corner of the screen for days, in the same spot it never moved. I took pictures, showed friends, and then someone said, "In Hawaii, it symbolizes a deceased loved one who is visiting." When I returned home, the large black moth was gone. Was it really Chad, or was that just something I needed to believe?

Since then, my antenna is always up looking for signs in almost everything... the birds that sit on my lanai railing, the heart-shaped coral I find at the beach, heart shapes in the ripples of the ocean waters, the humpback whales that give birth to new life in Hawaiian waters, the white fluffy figure that forms in the brilliant blue sky, the interesting people I meet, and the sea turtles that crawl up the beach and sleep within a few feet of me.

I think of Chad a lot and remember the signs of our love. He would wrap his long, strong arms around me and quickly pulse his hugs, which created a strange high pitched screech that would explode from my mouth. Once we started laughing the burst of sounds were different with every pulse. Remembering the love in his eyes and in his deep voice puts a smile on my face. His intoxicating smell will forever be imbedded in my memory. When Chad would make a far-fetched statement, he would slightly lift one corner of his closed mouth. I would look him square in the eye and do an exaggerated version. He would laugh and say, "I don't do that!" Occasionally Chad would stare at large-breasted women and when he got caught, he would say, "I'm conducting an experiment." I would smile, laugh, and reply, "Yeah, okay!" It became an ongoing joke after a popular pizza commercial. When either of us saw a large-breasted woman we turned to each other and one of us would say, "She sure has a lot of pepperoni in her bread." The many times he started to kiss me and would swiftly lick my nose with his sloppy wet tongue. I miss every sign!

We had only been dating a few months when he told me, "I'm chunk of coal, but will be a diamond someday." The day we married, he told me how happy he was and what a wonderful life we would have together. Every day he told me he loved me more than anything, even while he was going through radiation and chemotherapy. He told me by snuggling up to me in his hospital bed before his death.

Some of the signs (maybe a dream, or someone I briefly chatted with at a store checkout, a book I read, or a phone conversation with a friend) are not always immediately

151

recognized. It may take days, weeks or even months to put the pieces together.

Did Chad put Logan in my life so I could help him, at the same time helping me to heal?

Chad always promoted independence and took the initiative to repair things himself. Once upon a time, our washing machine stopped working and instead of calling a repairman, Chad went to the library and checked out a home repair book. It walked him through the diagnostic steps, and he determined the timer was broken. He removed the timer mechanism, dropped it at a repair shop, and reinstalled it. He was very proud of what he did, and it saved hundreds of dollars. Chad didn't like to ask for help, unless it was absolutely necessary. When the attempt at the boat motor repair was not a success, he took it to a qualified mechanic. He always thought having brakes replaced on the cars was outrageously expensive, so he had a friend teach him and he started replacing brakes on our cars. Don't mistake a learning experience for cheapness; Chad was not cheap.

Chad used the word "tough" often... "be tough, don't let things get to you" and "be tougher, you can do it." I clench my teeth now... he was tough. Chad would not complain about anything, physically anyway. He felt if he did complain he was a wimp. I was somewhat like that, it came from years of military service, so I understood. A soldier does not complain, they are strong, mentally and physically. In basic training my entire platoon went down for push-ups when one person complained. I remembered doing 500 in one day, thanks to several mouthy soldier buddies. Chad and I didn't complain about having a cold, headache, being sore from a workout, or some type of injury, it just wasn't in our makeup. When he was diagnosed with Stage IV cancer that had spread to his bones, the doctor asked, "How have you been able to tolerate such bone pain?" Chad looked him in the eye and said, "I just did it." I learned there is a time, a place, and sometimes a good reason to complain.

Perspective, as defined in the American Heritage Dictionary:

1. a. A view or vista.

   b. A mental view or outlook: "It is used occasionally to look at the past to gain a perspective on the present." (Fabian Linden)

2. The appearance of objects in depth as perceived by normal binocular vision.

3. a. An understanding of how aspects of a subject relate to each other and to the whole: a   perspective of history, a need to view the problem in the proper perspective.

   b. Subjective evaluation of relative significance; a point of view.

   c. The ability to perceive things in the actual interrelations of comparative importance: tried to keep my perspective throughout the crisis.

When I hear the word "perspective," it reminds me of both my old life and my new life, and then I compare the two. But that's not really fair, is it? My life is my life, and it's different now. Allowing perspective means I put parts of my life in their proper place, seeing life more clearly. Some things are not as important now, or have more or less significance. I have a short amount of time on earth to enjoy all the wonderful things – friends, family, adventures, incredible scenic beauty, and everyday experiences. On the other hand, there are other not-so-pleasant things that have descended on me, which have helped me to become conscious that each of us lives with our own issues. Losing Chad has left me with a new outlook... what is truly important in my life? For each one of us the answer will be different. My new perspective is that if problems do not carry a life or death consequence, my precious energy is not burned to the ground by them. By allowing this, my attitude is more positive and I carry less stress, which ultimately provides me with extra time and energy to focus on the deeper meaning of my life.

Life really sucks sometimes, but looking around it's even worse for someone else.

Chapter 25

HOMELESS, HUNGRY, AND THE LESS FORTUNATE

I locked my car and walked across the street to an oceanfront county park. The sprawling green lawn ended at a short black-lava rock wall, which bordered a beautiful beach. There were two large boats just offshore, shifting back and forth with the waves. Just a little further out, a humpback whale breached and white water exploded like a fountain. As I looked around, four guys stood under a tree smoking; the smell of marijuana floated through the air.

A big white-paneled truck pulled up to the curb and a few young adults jumped out of the back. We greeted each other with hugs and smiles, then unloaded tables, coolers, bins of supplies, and trays of food. As we set up the meal line, people gathered and formed a line in front of us. Many seemed to know each other and they smiled, hugged, and conversed. Others appeared to be loners; they didn't talk and they stared at the ground.

For a few months now I'd been helping Ardie and his wife, Jan, with their program, "Task Force on Feeding the Hungry." At least once a week and sometimes twice a week I helped serve free meals to those in need. Over time I got to know several of them by name, and they knew me.

Roger told me, in an excited voice as his hands flipped around in front of his face, how his identity had been stolen and everyone on the island now used his name and made charges to his credit card. He had tried many times to resolve the issue through his bank, but they would no longer talk to him. He asked for my help.

Jamie, in her mid-thirties, held her newborn baby girl as she explained how she was trying to clean up her life so she could get custody of her six-year-old son. Then she told me her father was a doctor and visited twice a year; he would arrive tomorrow. She provided the details of her college drug days, where she experimented with too many drugs and now had memory issues. But without hesitation she rattled off every twenty-letter ingredient on a box of granola bars. She pulled out a large white towel from the baby's stroller and told me how she planned to cut it up and use it for diapers.

John cruised in almost every week on his bike, but one evening he rolled in on skates. When I asked him what was up, he explained that his bike had a flat tire and he was hungry. After that meal, I dropped him off at Walmart so he could purchase a tire repair kit. John recently returned from Alaska where he had checked on his house – neighbors told him his crack dealer tenants had destroyed it. Some time ago he invented a sustainable energy refrigeration device, and recently had me video him on his cell phone. He then submitted the piece to various trade organizations hoping someone would help him produce, market, and sell the device. He slept in his storage container.

Ken bought papayas daily from a lady at the farmer's market; she would sell him several that were too ripe for only one dollar. He wrote stories for the Air Force Times magazine and was working on a book. Ken spent his days at the beach and evenings at McDonald's, where he had access to free Wi-Fi. He had recently moved because a homeless crackhead, as he described him, stole his stuff. But no worries, he found a tree that was partly hollow – he slept well in there and didn't get wet when it rained. He told me to stop by sometime and check it out.

The Sergeant Major came every week with an American flag draped around his shoulders. His fingernails were always painted and he carried a beautiful animal print bag. Sometimes he talked about his military service, where he was stationed, and the Vietnam War. One morning he was found dead behind the post office.

Carrie stumbled towards me with her arms open, gave me a warm hug, and slurred out, "I love you." Through her blank stare and abnormally large pupils, she asked what food was being served tonight, then showed me the beautiful necklace around her neck. She made it. I had not seen her in a couple of weeks; she said she was getting three meals a day and a warm bed to sleep in. She had been in jail.

John had to be six-and-a-half feet tall; you didn't miss him in a crowd. He always wanted to show me the amazing pictures he had taken and the stunning art work he created. I would often see him sitting on the pier in town where he would etch or write, and I would stop just to smile and say hi. He slept under a tarp in an empty field.

I didn't know most of their names, but I knew what they liked. One was a vegetarian, another preferred fruit and salad, one liked desserts, no carbohydrates for him, she loved chocolate, and several came back for seconds.

As Ardie blessed the food, people took off their hats and bowed their heads. The first gentleman in line was a regular and dressed the same every week: yellow baseball hat; short-sleeve, grey t-shirt; and dark denim jeans. He never looked at me when I handed him a plate of food and I didn't know if he was shy, or maybe embarrassed? I watched as he found a place on the lawn, sat down under a shady tree, and took his first bite. I wondered if it was his first meal of the day, or the week.

Leftover food was always given away, and I was awarded that job. They told me I was good at it. I loaded up a brown cardboard box with bread, cookies, drinks, or whatever was left and walked around the park. Faces lit up and some held out their soiled hands and accepted the food. All replied "God bless," or "thank you." One lady in her mid-fifties approached and asked for something to drink. When I handed her a bottle of soda, she started to cry. I placed my arms around her and asked her what was wrong. She replied, "Nothing, I was just thirsty." I handed her two more bottles of soda; she cried harder.

I can't imagine living every day like this... hungry, thirsty, and spending the night on the beach or under an easement of a building until the police chased you away.

My body filled to overwhelming levels with extreme gratification... but why? I only gave two hours a week, and to me it was a small thing. But for some of the people who came for meals it was the moon, the stars, and beyond. Many sought me out on that day, because I paid attention. Most times I didn't say a word... just smiled, listened, and gave a hug; it was a gift to them. When it wasn't meal day, I bought some of them ice cream cones, gave away my leftovers as I walked out of a restaurant, handed out Subway gift cards, gave rides, and bought sandwiches at a local store to give to one of them on the street. There's a sense of fulfillment that comes from inside that motivated me to continue. I received immense satisfaction to be involved in the lives of every person I encountered. It gave me a greater understanding of my duty to help others, particularly those who are less fortunate. My gift each week was a heartfelt gesture and knowing I made a small difference. But what I walked away with outweighed my gift one hundred-fold. I now had a greater appreciation for the human race, diversity, tolerance, and patience.

The perception that volunteering was something you do for nothing was far from the truth. I've gained things money can't buy – personal growth, appreciation of life and what I have, living in the moment, being more grateful, and loving myself for who I am and what I have to offer. The satisfaction, pride, and inspiration I received has made me a better person and my life is richer for it. And I learned that I can impact my life and others' lives. With this knowledge, I am capable of anything.

Chapter 26

RENOVATIONS

When I thought about home repairs maintenance, and renovations, a man always came to mind. Do men have a unique gene that gives them special knowledge about home projects? How do they just know this stuff? At this point in my life, I barely knew how to work a screwdriver, let alone power tools. My skill level consisted of hanging pictures, painting the walls, or rearranging furniture. Advancing my skill set was never something I wanted to do, because I didn't need to. I had Chad.

After talking to several contractors and the sticker shock of the quotes, I hoped to save money by doing my own renovations. After weeks of watching various home improvement videos, I decided to go for it. It didn't look hard or too technical; I believed I could do it. My confidence was lifted even further after talking to specialists at a home improvement store. My countless questions were answered and they convinced me I could do this. One even said, "If my sixty-five-year-old grandmother can do it, so can you."

That's all I needed to hear. Give me a challenge, I accept. Living on an island meant the variety of in-stock options were slim, so I had to special order most of my supplies. But on the upside, it gave me a couple of weeks to prepare.

In the meantime, I bought a pry bar and lifted one corner of the dingy green high-pile carpet in my condo and pulled as hard as I could. From there I ripped up and cut off small sections, rolled it, taped it, and carried it down three flights of stairs, continuing until all six hundred feet of carpet were lying in the metal dumpster. My groundwork had begun, and as the days went by I got more and more excited. I always liked a challenge and hit it head-on with a gutsy attitude. A little stress was good, too… it would push me just a bit harder and a bit further, until I conquered the challenge, possibly even surpassing my goal.

I was leaning against the passenger side of my SUV at contractor pick-up, in front of the home improvement store, when a massive white pick-up truck pulled up behind me. John, a contractor who had given me a quote, jumped out of his truck, "What are you doing?" he asked.

"Awaiting my renovation supplies," I replied.

He grinned and chuckled.

"You are not getting everything into that," he said as he pointed to my small SUV.

"I'll have to make a few trips," I answered. "This is the only vehicle I have."

He walked away mumbling something and within ten minutes a forklift appeared with a huge load. It was my flooring and bathroom supplies. At John's request, the forklift driver put everything on his big white truck. John was a very generous man, or as many would say, "It was the Hawaiian way." John and his crew followed me to my condo

161

and even helped me carry everything to the third floor. Who does that?

My plan… to start with the bathroom – rip out the toilet, vanity, and floor. When that was complete I would lay the wood floors throughout the rest of the condo. It would look amazing when I finished.

After I inventoried my supplies, I rolled up my sleeves and went to work. In an attempt to turn off the water under the vanity in the bathroom, I was forced to use the gentle persuasion of a claw hammer, complete with teeth gritting and gut grunting, which, despite my best effort, resulted in a slow continuous water leak. What have I done?! My frustration and ignorance to the situation was crushing, and I tossed my hammer onto the bathroom floor, pushed my back up against the tub as I sat on the floor, and cried. What now? I was used to being self-sufficient, and when I couldn't be… I had Chad. Chad would know exactly what to do in this situation. I was not going to give up, however, because my willpower to learn and do it myself was strong, but I needed to recognize that sometimes it required help… the help of a professional. I called a plumber. As I wrote out the check and thanked him several times, he asked me who was going to renovate my bathroom. I smiled with conviction and replied, "me."

After all the stress, anger, and frustration of the water leak – tearing the doors off the vanity and beating the side with a hammer, as pieces of wood went flying, was extremely gratifying. Once I let go of the negativity, the renovation moved along without a hitch.

I carefully read the directions of the wet tile saw, and felt somewhat confident about using this cutting machine. It said to place it on a solid surface, so the kitchen counter was good. I filled the trough to the indented line with water, just as the instructions said. On went the goggles. I reached for the power switch and hesitated. "Oh, come on, Leah, don't be a wimp!" I flipped the switch and immediately a loud whirling noise pierced my ears. I filled my lungs with air, relaxed my shoulders on the exhale, and placed the ceramic tile on the cutting table. As I slowly moved it towards the blade, my heart pounded faster. This was exhilarating – the power, the noise, the dirty hands, the perfect cut. I now see why men love their power tools.

As rough as this imperfect project started out, it was a smooth finish. It was such a feeling of accomplishment, particularly since I had never considered doing anything like this before. I thought it would be too complicated and above my skill level. Despite this, I believed I could do it and continued to move forward and asked for help when I needed it. It was stressful. It was aggravating. It was intimidating at times. But it was my accomplishment!

The next job was laying six hundred square feet of wood floors, which had a few challenges, but nothing major. I continued to throw hand tools, and walk away from the work to clear my head. My sore hands and knees didn't keep me from plowing through, day after day. Progress was slower than I had anticipated, but I finally finished. It was beautiful. The renovations helped me overhaul myself... build confidence in my abilities, believe in myself even though I had no clue what I was doing, and learn to ask for help. Every decision came with some daily strain, but well worth the learning experience.

Some of my rookie choices were not the best, and I quietly beat myself up. But when I thought about what I did, I was pleased with myself. I looked up and said, "How does it look Chad? I did it." Tears filled my eyes as I knew he would be proud, and he would brag to everyone, "Look what Leah did."

Chapter 27

THE TWO-YEAR MARK

On the second year of Chad's death, my text message alert on my cell phone went off at 3:30am. Normally I would put my phone on silent before I went to bed, but I didn't on this night. Should I look or not? I might as well, I was already awake. I grabbed my phone off the night stand and stared at the screen until it was clear enough to read. My heart skipped a beat when I saw it was from my BFF's husband and immediately thought something was wrong with her or their family. As I read the message, tears rolled down my face. It was my dear friend Charlie, his wife's obituary. What? That couldn't be. Suddenly my text alert dinged again, this time from another friend in Syracuse, she asked, "Have you talked to Charlie lately?"

I forced my numb body out of bed and paced around for twenty minutes. What should I do? Should I call Charlie or text him? What happened? Could I help? Was he okay? I was overloaded... angry, confused, tearful, and restless. I needed to unload some of my emotions, so I put on my running clothes and pounded the pavement before sunrise. I ran faster and faster as my mind focused on death... Chad, my dad, Chad's dad, anticipation of my mom, brother, even me, and Renee (Charlie's wife). My dad struggled with cancer for five years and it ripped my heart out to watch. Chad's dad shot himself in the head so he would not be a burden to his family, which angered me initially, but now I understand. Charlie's wife did the same unthinkable deed, in their home. How will he continue to live there?

I started thinking about what would happen when my mom dies. Thinking about my family slowly disappearing. Death knows no age... babies, toddlers, teenagers, young men/women, middle aged, and elderly.

After three miles, I sat down on a picnic table on the beach and stared out into the ocean. I put in ear buds and turned on some music. For the next hour, I sat and continued to stare, trying to focus while I inhaled, exhaled, and counted and controlled each breath.

As I ran the three miles back home, the stress was not as severe. My mind, body, and behavior had pushed away the heavy burden. I had to again accept the situation, learn and grow from it. It's the wave of grief I was thrown back into, but why on this day, exactly two years later?

I attempted to escape the intense emotions, called a few friends, talked to my mom, went to the gym, and saw a movie at the theater. Nothing seemed to help for long. That evening I found myself sitting at an oceanfront bar. The emotional pain had returned to an overwhelming level and I didn't want to be alone. Death is the end of our time on Earth. Death is inevitable, for all of us. Death is frightening. Death has taken people I love and made me feel empty inside, like my heart and soul had been removed and an endless, gaping black hole remained. I ordered one drink after another... I drank, and drank and drank massive amounts of alcohol. It was a way to forget. It eased the anxiety, and soothed the pain, for a few hours anyway. Finally, it was last call. I paid my bill and walked to the parking lot.

As I sat down in the driver's seat, all I could do was cry. Why was death hitting me so hard today? Had I not already been through most of the grieving process? What was it about a middle-age woman's death that sent me over the edge? Or, was it more about what Charlie was going through, and knowing how tough survival could be at times? I empathized, but also did not understand everything I was feeling. I dried my tears, started my car, and drove the half-mile home, which I absolutely should not have done. That was really stupid, Leah!

I pulled into a parking spot at my condo complex and turned the air conditioning on high... I wasn't feeling very well. With my eyes closed, I slumped over the console and laid my head on the passenger seat and fell asleep. Sometime later I woke up with a pain in my right side, from the console that had been jammed into my ribs. As I slowly sat upright everything seemed to move, my chest and abdomen had a warm sensation and my mouth began to water. I grabbed the door latch and pushed open the car door just as projectile vomit spewed from my mouth. I finally turned the ignition off and carefully stretched my right leg across the mess on the pavement, and staggered across the parking lot, falling into the stairwell railing. With both hands, I grasped the railing to steady myself, slinging my purse over my shoulder and slowly walking up to the third floor. I hoped and prayed no one was watching; I was mortified.

As I entered my condo, nausea swept over me again and I ran for the toilet. It felt like my insides were being shredded and spit out. When I was finished vomiting, I removed every piece of clothing from my sweltering body, curled up in the fetal position, and fell asleep on the cool tile floor.

When I opened my eyes the next morning, my head was heavy, it throbbed and felt like it had cracked open. I rolled onto my back, placing both palms on the floor and pushed myself up to a seated position. I felt miserable. My legs were shaky and unstable as I stood and looked in the mirror. Who was this person with blood shot eyes and mascara streaks down her face? I closed my eyes and took in a deep breath... you weren't very smart, Leah.

My insides were raw and on fire. My head throbbed each time I blinked my eyes and it felt like a knife had been jabbed through my right eye. I stretched out on the couch and slept off and on all day, while the television quietly played. I was afraid to eat or drink anything, and didn't, for hours. But finally, I sipped water and was able to choke down two crackers and some ibuprofen. I hoped to feel better the next morning.

What was I thinking? It took me two days to recover from that escapade. As I started to feel better I felt shame, humiliation, and embarrassment. I felt like a complete idiot. In a desperate attempt to dull the extreme pain I had turned to alcohol, which I had never done before. It only masked my feelings with the self-infliction of a temporary fix, which made me feel awful for a different reason. Alcohol is everywhere and people drink it for different reasons. I don't need alcohol... I can talk to strangers without it, have fun without it, and it's not my liquid courage. For some it's a reward, because they had a bad day at work, or they're stressed, or think they deserve it because their life sucks. I don't drink at all now, and I don't know if this will be for my lifetime, or if it's just a phase. For now, I found a different way to reward myself... a manicure, pedicure, massage, or reading a good book on the beach.

I was not immune to grief and powerful emotions, even two years later. Grief can be messy, with no timeline and no rules. I didn't deal with it perfectly, but I now understand there are other ways, better ways, healthier ways, ways that honor my grief, honor myself, and honor those who are deceased.

Chapter 28

NEW SOCIAL LIFE

Moving to a new city was difficult and building relationships from scratch was scary. It was the countless questions; I feared that people would eventually pin me into a corner while I tightly gripped my secret. Do I tell it, ignore the question, or somehow skirt around it?

I randomly selected a hair salon from the yellow pages, and when I called for an appointment I chose the stylist with the first available opening. Suzi was about my height and in her early forties, cute with long blonde hair and a tan; she was a surfer. Suzi was born and raised in Philadelphia and Chad had grown up one hour west of there; it was where he sought cancer treatment.

That was the start of my bond with Suzi, but little did I know that it was a horrific day for her. Chills crept up my spine as I quietly sat in the salon chair. Five years to the day, Suzi's husband Frank had passed away after a short fight with pancreatic cancer. I held my breath as she told me that they had two small children at the time of his death, and she had been a stay-at-home mom. She felt trapped and overwhelmed in her large home, surrounded by lots of property, and there was a mortgage. Tears streamed down my cheeks as I gazed into the mirror in front of me and stared into Suzi's face. As I walked out of her shop that day, a rush of grief overwhelmed me as my partially healed heart began to crack open again.

Despite this, my appointments became therapy sessions. As Suzi trimmed my hair, we cried and told stories from our past and details of our current lives... the waves of grief, the struggles to move on, and the heartache of missing the unconditional love we once had. We would often smile and say to each other, "Chad and Frank put us on the same path to meet each other."

There was an electric energy that excited me when I saw her, and that comfortable excitement drew me closer. I didn't feel judged or labeled by anything I said, because Suzi shared many of the same thoughts and fears. We both desired to love and to be loved, and for those shared moments, we showed love to each other. Each time we parted ways we wrapped our arms around one another in a warm, firm hug, our hearts pressed into each other's chest, caressing our deeply shared pain. Somehow the embrace calmed me and a fresh flicker of renewed force filled my body.

Even though I hadn't known her long, the sense of closeness to Suzi was invaluable. She showed me how to be comfortable with my secret, to share it in a healing way, and to understand that there were other people in the world with similar feelings and losses. We were not alone. I was not alone.

I met people everywhere – Hawaii was just that way. I visited the local gyms, and then joined one. Once a week I grabbed a table at a local coffee shop, read, ate breakfast, and hung out. People started to recognize me as a frequent guest, and we struck up conversations. I read the daily paper, joined email newsletters, and combed the internet for local events. I attended everything – art gallery openings, "Words and Wine" at a local bookstore, writers' workshops, comedy shows, plays, film festivals, arts and craft shows, parades, and concerts. I met friendly and genuine people wherever I went. We exchanged stories and eventually phone numbers. People invited me on hikes, to dinner at their house, or for an afternoon at the beach. Some were comfortable enough to ask me to house and dog sit. I never turned down a social invitation; it was my way of meeting more people. Sometimes I would inconvenience myself for the sake of a social life or a new friend.

One new friend, Melody, had been recently diagnosed with breast cancer. In the weeks prior to her surgery I grew closer to her; I wanted to help and be a caring friend. I would stop by her house just to say hi. I told her that if she needed anything, day or night, to call me. Melody looked great on the outside, but that dreadful disease had begun to eat its way into her otherwise healthy body. I needed to believe that my presence somehow made a small difference to her. I tried to act normal. I didn't want to turn into that rambling nervous friend who made strange remarks or was uncomfortably silent. But occasionally my fears were overwhelming… cancer had again inserted itself into my life. What would I say to Melody? Could I pretend to be comfortable, like everything was okay? At times, I found that to be a real struggle. The word "cancer," and visions of a sick Chad floated around in my head and I fought to keep those thoughts in check. Not everyone would struggle like Chad had, and not everyone would have the same outcome he did. For brief moments with Melody I had the usual thoughts – we talked about her day at work, her new boyfriend, and her grandkids. But then a flush of reality… she was sick. It felt like my emotions were being squeezed through a ringer. Could I handle this?

The morning of Melody's surgery I woke up in a panic. I was going back to a hospital. Could I do it? But as badly as I wanted to stay safe in the confines of my home that morning,

I did not allow myself. I gently tucked my fears into a small place in the back of my mind. As I pulled opened the front door to the hospital, the cool air-conditioned air chilled me to the bone. I nervously wound my way through the maze of hallways, staring at the familiar shiny white tile floor as the lights beamed down on me. Only occasionally did I look up for a sign, to point me in the right direction.

When I finally arrived in the waiting room, it was filled with other friends and Melody's loving daughters. Melody had a courageous smile and a spirited attitude, which made me feel better. My friend with cancer made ME feel better. How ironic is that?

This reminded me of a friend in Syracuse. She and I had dinner together right before I moved to Hawaii. She was genuinely unhappy and had been for months due to her dysfunctional family, her disrespectful siblings, and her messed up marriage. She had been with Chad and me during the good times as well as the tough times. That night at dinner I took her hand and leaned into the table. She looked me in the eye when I said, "I wish you could be as happy as I am right now." What was it about a friend being sad for valid reasons, and a friend in the deep trenches of a grave situation mustering up enough interest to provide comfort?

I snapped back into the moment when the nurse called Melody's name, and she asked if her friends – Pam, Connie, and I – could go back to pre-op with her. The nurse obliged. The three of us stood around Melody as she lay in a hospital bed. She pulled down the top of her gown and pointed to the tattoos the doctor had put on her chest, and explained what would happen during surgery. My stomach tightened, my palms were sweaty, and I suddenly felt ill. The visual was more than I could take… her bare chest, the gown, the white sheets, the hospital bed, the IV, the tubes, and the monitoring equipment. With a lump in my throat the size of a baseball, I tried to push the tears and anxiety back. Just then a nurse walked in and wheeled Melody towards the surgery room. I waved my quivering hand as she disappeared around the curtained wall.

That day brought back many uncomfortable feelings... being frightened of the outcome, feeling terrified in a hospital setting, the concern on everyone's face. As difficult as it was, I waited patiently with everyone else. I found that my idle mind was my worst enemy and I fought to keep my emotions intact. I resisted the urge to go home and crawl into bed, I avoided the terrifying thoughts of my dying Chad, and I refused to think that would happen to Melody. Some chose to stay clear of the uneasy hospital scene... why did I put myself in the middle? Because I wanted to. I wanted to prove my fears were weaker than my desires to support a friend in need.

We all travel down our own road towards an unknown destination. The road is not always smooth, and we encounter many challenges on the way. We stumble, fall, and crawl our way through as our strengths and weaknesses are tested. Sometimes we cross paths with others and sometimes we need to stop and pick that person up, let them pick us up, or open ourselves to a whole new world.

A friendly couple who lived in my complex told me about a local gathering every Friday during happy hour. I went one Friday and met Nora. Growing up our lives were similar – our dads were in the military so we moved around a lot as kids, and our families were from the South. Early in our relationship, Nora told me the details of her divorce and how she wished she would have done it years ago... all the while I never told my secret and she never asked. I was a good listener, that way there was no fear my secret would be leaked. One evening over dinner Nora said, "People have their story and it's their story to tell." She was comfortable telling me about her life and I had to reciprocate, otherwise there would be no friendship. I knew at that moment I needed to put myself out there – open up my secret and be vulnerable; it was the only way to deepen our connection.

Nora patiently listened as my eyes filled with tears; she leaned into the table and said, "Leah, I'm really sorry for your loss and what you had to go through." A public restaurant was not the choice I would have made to disclose the toughest point in my life, but the time was right. Nora and I locked eyes as she asked a few questions, but then quickly changed the subject. She never felt sorry for me, or made me feel uncomfortable. As a matter of fact, it was the opposite – I felt normal with Nora. I did not have to hide anything or wonder if she judged me or what she thought of my actions or feelings. Because it didn't matter, we were forever friends.

Nora provided support even when she couldn't help me... like the time we walked in the Relay for Life. I cried as I walked around the track in a state of bewilderment; she walked by my side and didn't say a word, she was just there. Nora was like my sister; she made me feel at ease. We laughed, we cried, we got cranky, we were positive people looking for positive outcomes no matter how tough the circumstances. When we hung out together, it was like an amusement park – everyone wanted to join us. It was a happy place wherever we went, a joyful time no matter day or night. We ignited the fun in each other. I enjoyed the zero to sixty in 1.3 seconds, which is how fast we made up our minds to do something. And, the thrill of dangling our feet off a sea cliff while we watched the sun set was about as crazy as it got. Road trips on the island were fairly frequent; a music festival, rodeo, Fourth of July fireworks, or a chilly rainy weekend in the Rain Forest. Without guilt, fun and excitement had again entered my life, and it felt good; it put a smile on my face and made me happy. Sometimes just being around people was enough; they didn't have to be friends or even acquaintances. Just a friendly person's presence was enjoyable and soothing to my soul.

Dance has long been known as a social activity and a way to lift the spirit. It was also a means of expressing myself in way I had never done before, and I loved music. The first group lessons were intimidating; my lack of experience made me uncomfortable. How did I look... was I too stiff, did I move with the beat? At home I would dance in front of the mirror, that way I could see what I was doing or not doing. Dance was not complicated, but sometimes I made it that way by focusing too much on my feet and not enough on the rhythm of the music. "Don't be so serious, Leah! Just enjoy!" Through weekly lessons my skills became noticeably more refined and my confidence soared. But there was one more hurdle – I felt extremely awkward when face to face with a man who was a stranger. As soon as he reached for my hand, my body stiffened. I held his warm hand and gently laid my left hand in the middle of his back... our bodies were only inches apart, and we stared into each other's eyes. What was he thinking? All I wanted to do was squirm, let go of his hand, and walk away, but I forced myself to relax and resist the impulse. "Just enjoy and learn, Leah!" Everyone took lessons for different reasons and none of us criticized, mocked, or made fun of anyone. Most of the dancers were extremely friendly and asked me to lunch, or to take in a movie, or attend a party. Dance kept my body and brain active and increased my self-esteem and confidence. It was something I could continue to get better at, and it was a new way to enjoy myself. But would I ever be at ease in the arms of another man, no matter how innocent?

Over time I truly came to enjoy the company of my female friends. There was no awkward moment at the end of the evening... was she going to kiss me, or did she expect an invite back to my place? Plus, I didn't have to get my "brutally honest" attitude out. I DO NOT want a romantic relationship. For some men, they never got it. Were they persistent or just ignorant?

After being friends for a few months, one guy increased his calling, texting, and emailing, to a point where I felt uncomfortably harassed. Just because we shared Dutch dinners once in a while did not mean we were dating. He knew my secret, because I told him. He shared his, the death of his son. But that did not make us soul mates. I continued to tell him, "I'm not interested in a romantic relationship with you or anyone else. If you cannot be friends, we're done." Then he would back off for a few days or a week, but his communication eventually increased to a disturbing level... he would text many times a day and if I did not immediately respond, his texts became obsessive, ten in one minute. His actions scared me. What if he was a deranged lunatic? I had never even held this guy's hand, let alone anything more romantic. What did he not get? I had to finally call the authorities, they contacted him and his communication ceased. Maybe I was the ignorant one? Can guys be friends with a female, or do they always want more?

One guy I briefly met through a mutual friend... we talked at a concert only because we sat next to each other, while his girlfriend sat on the other side of him. He asked if I was single, where I worked, and where I lived. Two days later my condo manager knocked on my door. The guy from the concert came to my complex looking for me and when the manager would not divulge my unit number, he left a note: "Great to meet you Leah, call me sometime." It was signed with his name and phone number. That was creepy and he had a girlfriend! His actions made me feel like a chunk of meat hanging from a hook, "Oh, I'll take that one please! Can you wrap it to go?"

Obviously, I did not call him.

On the other hand, some guys were great. We could enjoy lunch, dinner, a hike, or watch a college basketball game, with no strings attached. One of them told me, "Leah, most men are like monkeys. They swing from a vine, and as they swing back and forth they look around for a better vine, and when they see one, they make a leap." Are they not comfortable being alone, or are they insecure? There was no room in my life for such behavior.

Along the way, I've met many wonderful people in Hawaii with whom I've shared numerous conversations, holidays, a dance, a sunset, a meal, beach time, and a laugh. I have given some of them rides to work, computer repair support, delivery service, taxi service, and garden sitting. Each person has brightened my day, and helped me to realize there are many things in my life to be grateful for.

Meeting new people and making new friends as an adult was not easy; even getting out of the house to meet new people was sometimes a challenge. But after meeting all these new people, I had someone to call if I wanted to go to a movie or have a day at the beach… it was now my choice to do it alone or not.

Chapter 29

WHERE I FIND PEACE

Life is difficult enough, why make it more so?

Me Time

I struggled to carry a fabric chaise lounge with a metal frame up three flights of stairs; it was long, hinged, and the top part kept awkwardly flopping open, which made it a challenge to carry. Once I crossed the threshold of my front door it was a straight shot to the lanai. "Lanai" is defined in Merriam-Webster as, "a covered structure adjoining an entrance to a building – a low-slung Hawaiian beach house with an open-sided lanai to catch the tropical breezes."

I placed the lounge on the tile floor, unfolded it, and took the dangling tags and plastic off. I stepped inside and poured a large glass of cool water, grabbed my cell phone, a pen, and my journal. This was the space I created to be myself, grow within myself, and feel my emotions.

The sky was deep blue, almost purple, and not a cloud in sight. As I looked over the railing of my lanai, the turquoise Pacific Ocean disappeared into infinity and the gentle sound of the waves rolled into the short black lava wall that hugged the coastline and protected my home. The ocean water was so clear I could see several yellow tang swimming just below the surface. I was center stage as a pod of spinner dolphins performed an acrobatic show only fifty feet from the shore... one jumped straight up out of the water and twisted its body as it soared into the air. It then descended back into the water on its side. I closely watched the pod continue south along the coast until it disappeared into the distance.

I stretched out on my new chaise lounge as I gazed out over the ocean and took a deep breath. There was a slight breeze that danced between the swaying fronds on a nearby palm tree towering over me. Several saffron finches – small bright yellow birds with orange crowns – glowed against the lush green lawn below. A tiny green gecko inched its way across the tile to inspect my glass of water. The ocean air felt light, clean, and energizing. I picked up my pen, closed my eyes, and slowly relaxed every inch of my body. My mind let go of everything as the sound of the waves consumed me and I joined the free-flowing ocean energy. I filled my lungs with fresh salt water air and exhaled all the anxiety away. This was my nourishment for a calm and quiet moment.

I began to write in my journal... more than ever since the day he passed. I felt Chad holding my hand. His energy was peaceful, and our bond was strong. He was next to me, always by my side, and even though I couldn't see him I could feel him. He was here. Chad let me experience so many things and I am grateful for them all – life, love, happiness, heartache, and endings. It was my choice, what I did with these feelings and emotions. I desperately wanted to live life and never wanted to avoid it. I wanted to live with love and happiness, not with anger and despair. I continued to write...

If I did not know how, I chose to learn.

If I wanted to take a vacation, I chose to save my money until I had enough.

If I did not like looking at litter on the ground while walking in the park, I chose to pick it up.

If I wanted time alone, I chose to make the time.

The ocean waves reminded me of life – slow, relaxing, fresh, calm, peaceful, and therapeutic – as I floated on my back with my eyes closed. Then, when I least expected it, a massive, intense, and destructive rogue wave curled and crested over top of me, suddenly and unexpectedly crashing down upon me, forcing me deep under the water as I toppled head over heels, not knowing which way was up. I subconsciously held my breath while I flailed my arms in a desperate panic of survival as the waves continued to drag me further from shore. Would I be able to fight my way out of the grasp of Mother Nature? Could I hold my breath until I popped above the surface? Will another wave take me down? With those thoughts suspended in mid-air, a rush of panic warmed my body... where would I be a year from now? Would I survive the waves? What would I be doing? Did any of it really matter? Was any of it important? Yes... today WAS important, this moment was significant. I was ready to take on life, whatever it put in front of me. I am a survivor! It was all in my attitude, right?

My pen furiously traveled across the white lined paper... "What is peace?" It is the beauty that surrounds me, my self-worth, being true to myself and others, finding the good in people and situations, giving what I can, exploring the world, having passion in my heart. Smiling and laughing, even at myself. Being grateful. Accepting love. Knowing that I gave everything I could to Chad. There was nothing more I could have done; it was his time to go. I flipped through my journal until I found a quote I had written just a few days earlier: "We can never obtain peace in the outer world until we make peace with ourselves." ~Dalai Lama

Being immersed in my own thoughts brought out inner guidance. I'm comfortable with who I am, where I am, and the direction of my life. I love myself and value my opinion. I closed my eyes one more time, took in another deep breath, and absorbed the calm energy around me. My mind was clear and my energy renewed. I needed to remember that peace was always within me, regardless of the circumstances around me.

Living in Hawaii taught me to promote and respect all that is good for me. I used to have a seat on the high-speed train of life and when I looked out the window everything I passed was a blur… the trees were a distorted mess, the cars were a vague impression, and the flowers were not even noticeable. I see everything differently now. I don't just see the ferns, the flowers, and the birds – I now see the clear rain drop on the bright green fern and the almost invisible spider web that surrounds the red hibiscus. My awareness has shifted my vision from a black and white picture into a magnificent world of vibrant color and detail.

Connect with Nature

I thoroughly enjoy connecting with a life force that is much different from my own. One of my favorites is snorkeling at night with those gentle giants, the Manta Rays. The quiet and tranquility of connecting with the darkness of the massive ocean encourages calmness deep inside. Divers with large bright lights are in the water below me, attracting the plankton the mantas feed on. The gentle giants glide toward me – their six, seven, and eight-foot wing-like pectoral fins smoothly thrusting them through the vastness, and they swoop in around me. I give myself over to the ocean and the sea life. As the manta glides directly towards me with its mouth open, it suddenly performs a barrel roll and brushes its large cartilaginous body against my chest and torso. The rolling continues as it gathers a tasty snack of microscopic organisms. My immersed heart dances while watching this silent ballet, as the elegant, graceful beings express themselves on their stage. It's a magical energy that flows joy and vitality throughout my being.

Nature nurtures my soul. It has the unique ability to restore my inner peace. I receive guidance and wisdom as it brings me closer to my own spirit and the spirit of Chad. Nature heals, gives me meaning, and puts pleasure in my life.

Back on land, putting one foot in front of the other, I frequently travel a tranquil path into the forest, observing sounds, smells, creatures, and foliage. There's a damp chill in the air and the bright sun peeks through the dense forest canopy. My senses are captivated by the sound of the Coqui frogs serenading my every step, the whiff of decaying mangos that have fallen from a nearby tree, and the numerous unfurling of new ferns. As I journey along the uneven path I begin to hear a strong gush of rushing water... the winding path leads me to a gorgeous spot where the flowing water is at least twenty feet wide; it surges off the rocks from high above and then plunges, free falling, down the mountain, collecting in a serene pool at my feet. I sit down on a nearby rock and remove my shoes. I surrender to what is; I slowly maneuver my body into the cool water and connect to everything around me. I belong to the earth. Peace fills my overjoyed heart.

Remembering and Honoring

Chad wanted to celebrate his fiftieth birthday in South Africa, his favorite place on earth. I will go someday soon and take a few of his ashes, as he asked me to. Then he will forever be in the place he so loved.

There are days I want to go back, remember, and feel. I pick up Chad's obituary, written by his sister, and read all or parts of it: "Chad's karate expertise so impressed his nephews that they were completely convinced he could disable anyone using only one finger through the use of secret 'pressure points.' Chad also had a wicked sense of humor. When Leah and his sister-in-law Drew were attempting to stay dry during a particularly wet fishing expedition, he christened them 'Zsa

Zsa and Eva.' When discussing flying with a nervous first-time flyer, he assured her that 'you only have to worry if the crew starts explaining emergency procedures before take-off, because that means they are worried that the plane might crash.' Despite his many interests and accomplishments, Chad's greatest joy was his wife, Leah. He said during their wedding vows that he had met her when he was 'a lonely lieutenant.' With Leah as his wife, he was never lonely again, and knew the happiness of being married to the love of his life."

We had been dating a few months when Chad said, "I'm a chunk of coal, but will be a diamond some day." I knew he would always be my diamond.

The day we married in a small chapel in Las Vegas, Nevada, as tears of happiness streamed down my face, Chad told me how happy he was and what a wonderful life we would have together.

When he received a job transfer we loaded up our Chevy Blazer. With a canoe tied to the top and an eighteen-foot fishing boat in tow, we left Tacoma, Washington on a cool December morning and headed east. Chad bought me a down-filled winter coat and told me it was going to be a cold trip. I realized how cold when we stopped somewhere in the northwest for gas and was told by the attendant it was thirty below zero. Later that day, a state policeman closed the gate to the snow-covered highway as we passed him and headed up Deadman's Pass. Chad glanced at me and noticed the concern on my face. He said, "We will be fine," as he patted my left knee, and we were.

Chad promised to take care of me until death do us part, and he did just that.

One day while sitting on my lanai I unexpectedly noticed Chad's text messages on my cell phone. I had never thought about them before and a rush of excitement consumed me as I pulled up the last entry. I remembered pushing a grocery cart around the store when I received that text, "The pharmacy called, please check with them." I replied, "I will."

"When will you be home?" he asked.

This was my last text ever from Chad. Then I noticed the date – May 29, 2011, exactly one month prior to his death. My heart raced as I realized this was a tangible conversation I had carried around for two years. Why had I not seen or thought about this before? Then I looked for a voicemail message, but there was nothing. I longed for a recording, something I could play over and over again, just to hear the sound of his loving voice. But maybe that was Chad telling me it was probably not a good idea. I would save the previous text messages for another time when I needed a Chad conversation.

It's soothing to look at a picture of Chad and me and remember the moment... I smile. I enjoy telling stories about Chad, particularly funny ones... I laugh. Every part of my being fills with delight when I do something Chad would have loved... he's enjoying it with me. When I muster up the nerve to take on a challenging task I am proud because I know Chad would be too. Looking back on our incredible life together, I am grateful.

As the years go by, I am relieved to know Chad is still here, with me, in my heart. He watches from afar... he knows my struggles, sees my tears, and feels my happiness. Even though he can't physically kiss me and say, "I love you," I know he did and still does. I still hear him laugh while telling the skunk story. I still see the hurt in his eyes when he learned of his father's death. I still see the shock and concern on his face when he was rolled out of the emergency room to be admitted to the hospital. I still see him discussing life's lessons with his godson. Everything about him will be forever ingrained into my being... his loving eyes, his infectious smile, his scruffy face, his soft and gentle hands, and his intoxicating presence.

I still see Chad as larger than life, even though life knocked him out and dragged his unwilling body down the path of cancer and an early death. I still miss him, I still cry, it still hurts... and it will hurt every day of my life, but it's not that deep, sharp-edged pain I once felt. I have learned to live with the pain. Sometimes the door cracks open and the hurt steps out, but it's okay. I now know that I can experience those emotions and then close the door. The pain can freely come and go, but it will always have a home in the confines of that special place in my heart.

Chapter 30

FIRST DATE

He picked me up in his dark blue SUV, and was a complete gentleman. He opened the car door for me and waited until I drew my legs inside, then he gently closed the door and pulled on the handle to make sure the door was secure. How nice...

I couldn't keep my eyes off him as he slowly walked around the front of the car. His dark blue denim Levi's were fitted, showing off his nicely rounded butt. A light-blue, striped, collared shirt draped over his broad shoulders, and the sleeves were rolled up just below his elbows. His shirt was nicely tucked into his jeans with a brown leather belt wrapped around his trim waist. His head turned slightly to the left and his eyes darted briefly in my direction... was he checking to see if I was looking at him? He grinned and continued towards the driver-side door. My heartbeat radiated into my ears as he reached for his door handle; within a split second the door swung open and he sat down. His luscious/delicious scent drifted towards me as he closed his door. We both turned and looked at each other and smiled... my upper body tingled as we were inches apart. He looked away and inserted the key in the ignition, planted his foot on the brake, put the car in reverse, and softly placed his right hand on the back of my seat as he turned to check behind. My heart skipped a beat... he was close again and I could feel his breath in the air around me.

As he drove away from my home, he smiled and enthusiastically asked, "Do you like seafood?"

"Yes."

"I know the perfect place," he said.

I fidgeted in the passenger seat... crossed and uncrossed my arms, then settled in as I clasped my hands in my lap. I was nervous as I asked about his day, but he comfortably discussed his work and his brief workout at the gym. We pulled into a parking spot at the restaurant and he quickly got out, heading across the front of the car to my side... but I was already out of the car. He smoothly pushed the door closed behind me and extended his right arm as if to say – "walk this way." His actions made me feel special, like a princess. I smiled and said, "Thank you," as I slowly walked past him, my eyes connecting to his. My heart raced, by body tingled.

As we approached the front door of the restaurant he reached out and pulled open the door and I walked in. The hostess immediately escorted us to a table for two in a quiet corner of the dining room. He pulled out my chair as the hostess placed the menus on the table and then he took his seat directly across from me. We smiled. I felt awkward... where did I start?

I glanced down at the menu and asked, "What's your favorite food?"

"A good steak, fried chicken, and pizza," he replied.

We both picked up our menu and quickly decided.

We barely noticed our water glasses being filled and that bread was left on the table. Our attention was focused on each other. He had beautiful, thick, short dark brown hair and was clean shaven. His grey eyes were nothing like I had ever seen before; they shimmered with excitement. His striking smile was wide and happy. He placed his elbows on the edge of the table and leaned in slightly. My heart fluttered.

I hung to every word about his childhood, the horse farm he grew up on, working on the farm, high school football, his wrestling, and college. He talked about his grandparents, parents, and siblings... particularly about the rivalries. He was charming, confident, considerate, well spoken, and had a great sense of humor. As he told a couple of stories from his childhood, I laughed. He and his younger brother would play a game in the dark that consisted of a tennis ball at the bottom of a sock that they would swing around, hitting each other. "Really? Girls don't play those types of games," I joked. He also talked about getting into trouble and having to pick rocks out of the indoor riding arena as punishment. Once he cheated by putting rocks from the driveway into his bucket, but his dad was well educated on "rocks," and noticed the difference. Being caught red-handed he had to pick an additional bucket of rocks from the arena. He affectionately spoke about his love for the outdoors, the beach, and his family.

I was a little more reserved, and talked about my dad in the military and moving around as a kid. There were no bold stories about getting into trouble or what I did wrong. I didn't want him to judge me. After all, it was our first date.

He was a great listener... he didn't interrupt to give his point of view, or offer a solution. He didn't compare my middle-income life to his upper-income upbringing. He didn't interrogate or try to change the subject. He focused on me. Even through dinner we stared and focused on each other. No one else around us mattered. Neither of us scanned the room in boredom. It was as if we were the only two people there.

His eyes were warm and passionate. We were almost strangers, but I felt comfortable, and eager to know everything about this man. Was I one of those "love at first sight" believers? This was one of the most exciting yet terrifying dates I'd ever been on. My heart pounded hard most of the evening... butterflies flittered in my stomach... and somehow I knew, on that first date, that this was someone I could love.

The evening went by quickly and I so didn't want it to end. I wished for a pause button so I could spend more time with him, right now. I felt a powerful attraction.

As he walked me to my front door he said, "I had a wonderful time getting to know you." We stood at my door gazing into each other's eyes. He leaned into me and gently kissed me on my left cheek.

"May I call you again for another date?"

"Yes, Chad, I look forward to it."

Made in the USA
Columbia, SC
13 November 2021

48915103R00111